GERMANY

GERMANY

ARCHITECTURE · INTERIORS · LANDSCAPE · GARDENS

CHRISTA VON RICHTHOFEN · PHOTOGRAPHS BY OLIVER BENN

WEIDENFELD & NICOLSON · LONDON

Endpapers Wood inlay decoration on the walls of the Small Marquetry Chamber in the Neue Kammern at Sanssouci, Potsdam.

Page 1 Column detail in the Trinitatiskirche, Cologne.

Pages 2–3 Burg Hohenaschau, Bavaria.

Right The monastery library at Wiblingen, near Ulm, Baden-Württemberg.

First published in Great Britain in 1992 by George Weidenfeld & Nicolson Ltd, 91 Clapham High Street, London SW4 7TA

British Library Cataloguing-in-Publication Data
A catalogue record for this book is available from the British Library.

Translated by Eileen Martin
Captions (apart from Interiors Chapter) by Oliver Benn
Design by Helen Lewis
Map by Rita Wüthrich

Typeset by Keyspools Ltd, Golborne, Lancashire
Printed and bound in Italy

CONTENTS

ACKNOWLEDGEMENTS

The author and photographer are particularly grateful to Peter von Richthofen for all his assistance with their work.

They are also much indebted to Colin Grant, the publishers' editor, for his support and advice throughout the preparation of this book.

They would like to acknowledge the invaluable help and/or advice received from the following (listed in alphabetical order):

Schloßmuseum Arnstadt, Dr. Herwig Bartels, Julia Blunt, Friedrich und Hildegard von Bodelschwingh, Graf und Gräfin Clemens Droste zu Vischering, Dieter Diekmann, Karl Graf Eltz, Dr. Friedel Erhard, Freiburg im Breisgau Tourist Office, Freiherr und Freifrau Eccard von der Gablenz, Freiherr Carl August von der Gablenz, Cella-Margaretha Girardet, Schloßmuseum Gotha, Friedrich Gröning, Angelica Hack, Gerd Haferkorn, Dr. Martin Haushofer, Elisabeth von Herwarth, Gräfin Ingelheim, Heinrich Kaiser, Graf und Gräfin Carl-Albrecht von Kanitz, Karl-Josef Freiherr von Ketteler, Hans Kraske, Günther Kriegel, Landshut Tourist Office, Christiane Lessner, Dr. Regine Low, Lüneburg Tourist Office, Ingrid McAlpine, Elisabeth Maertens-Schwerin, Klaus und Pierre Mai, Dorothea von Moltke, Staatliche Schloßverwaltung Neuburg an der Donau, Prof. Dr. Nancy Netzer, Reinhard Querengässer, Hella Pick, Karl Rasche, Dr. Gabriele Rausch, Dr. Gottfried Riemann, Alexandra and Charles Roney, Hans-Joachim Roth, Petra Rottschalk, Oda Schoeller, Paul Graf Schönborn, Dr. Heinz Schönemann, Horst Schubert, Bernd Schulz, Elena Sollazzo, Roswitha von Studnitz, Bernhard Freiherr von Tucher, John Unwin, Sächsischer Verein für Volksbauweise, Graf und Gräfin von Wolff-Metternich zur Gracht, Staatliche Schlösser und Gärten Wörlitz.

The photographer and publishers are also very appreciative
of the generous assistance provided by P & O European Ferries
on two of the photographer's trips.

INTRODUCTION

*With reunification, Germany is once again embarking on a
journey of self-discovery in which all aspects of German
history and culture – such as the medieval cloister (above)
of the monastery church at Steingaden in Bavaria or the
Glienicke Bridge (opposite) in Berlin, on the former border
between East and West – will play a part.*

Germany in November 1989: A border guard stands with his back to the Berlin Wall, on a wooden crate to raise him above the crowd of people milling round him. He is desperately trying to get some sort of order into the surging mass. 'There are so many of you and only two of us!' he shouts, clearly on the defensive.

All of a sudden, they have become powerless, those East German border guards who had always been so threatening in their grey-green uniforms,

with their icy discipline and control. How often they had turned a car inside out on the inner-German border looking for refugees from their 'worker-peasant paradise' and acting with such precision. And now surely the sudden surrender must mean the end of the 'people's government'. The people were abandoning the regime, and no slogans could draw them back. These revolutionaries storming the Berlin Wall, the Bastille of the twentieth century, were ordinary citizens of a big city in jeans and parkas. But

at this moment their only desire was to breach the forbidding barrier that had locked them in for twenty-eight years. Their courageous and mighty demonstrations were about to topple a totalitarian regime that had become hollow and meaningless. This was a popular uprising that was being fought on the streets, but only with banners and slogans: 'Passports for everyone. Down with the Communist Party!', or simply 'We are the people!' And when this became 'We are one people', the whole of Germany

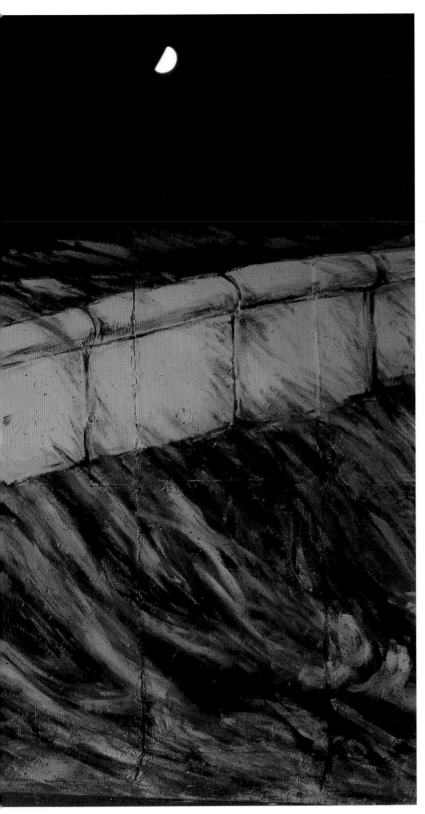

knew that unification had become unstoppable, and it was only a question of when it could be officially carried out.

Germany on 3 October 1990: The same, seemingly endless stream of people gathered before the Reichstag in Berlin, lit by the powerful floodlights from its roofs and towers flaring into the night sky. The unification ceremonies were performed with the whole world looking on. The emotions and hopes of the people were at one and the same time released and then drawn together when precisely at the stroke of midnight, the huge German flag was hoisted against the background of the flags of the individual sixteen German *Länder*.

The world with its television sets was able to share in that exuberant, breathtaking historic moment. It truly was a new beginning. But now the waves of pure emotion have given way to a more sober mood, and Germans are having to learn the hard way to overcome what had been the most bitter division in their history and to adjust to their new reality. A new unified whole will grow from the two parts that are now so different, and a new German identity will emerge. That the process will be difficult is clear from the fact that the Germans are still having problems deciding what to call each other. 'The former Federal Republic of Germany' and 'The former GDR' are temporary phrases. In popular speech the nicknames *Ossis* for the Easterners and *Wessis* for the Westerners have come into use. 'West Germany' and 'East Germany' are geographical

The Berlin Wall in Mühlenstrasse, Friedrichshain, which contains most of the Wall that is still standing. Much of it is covered with striking paintings that are both abstract and representational, like that of the crowd breaking through the Wall (left).

terms – how about the centre, the south and the north? These uncertainties and ambiguities will surely be resolved as the parts grow together again, but will it resolve the wider question of what is 'Germany' and what is 'German'?

I experienced such uncertainties as a child and as a refugee from the East. My family's fate was not unusual for that period. In 1945 and 1946 the whole of Germany was disintegrating, but the seeds of a new beginning had been planted.

My family had lived for many centuries in East Prussia, but had fled west from the war and approaching armies. My father was killed on the Eastern front in January 1945 and in December of that year the Soviet occupation troops commandeered the last property that had remained to us, which was near Berlin. My mother took her seven children and fled to West Germany. She was now without any means and was just one more of millions of refugees from the East. On the many stations of her journey she realized that she would have to start from scratch to build up a new life for herself and her children.

In the first few years after the war Germany seemed to be completely devastated, thrown back almost to the level of a pre-industrial agricultural land. To provide income for the family, my mother decided to start a market garden. The land she found came as a pure chance. In the Rhineland between Bonn and Cologne, there stood a wood of birch and pine. In 1946 it consisted in the main of stunted trees with thick undergrowth. It was home to many small wild animals and had been a favourite hunting ground of the last German Kaiser. The winter of 1946–7 brought Siberian temperatures, and need drove many shivering people from Bonn and Cologne into the wood with saws and axes in search of firewood. At first they furtively hacked off a few branches; then they grew bolder and bolder, and in the end only rough terrain was left; my mother was able to buy a few acres of it and started to cultivate blackberries.

I was six when my brothers and sisters and I moved into our new home, first into the cellar, since the house was being built at the time and construction work could only continue after my mother had been able to obtain building materials on the inevitable black market. From then on we children had to help in the garden and, depending on the season, dig up young shoots from the long parallel rows of brambles, cut back creepers and harvest the fruits.

My mother told us later that she made us all sing folksongs, while we were picking the fruit, to make sure the berries went into the baskets and not into our mouths.

Gradually she succeeded in establishing a reasonable level of prosperity for her family. For my mother, a widow and a refugee from the East, it was always a miracle that she had the opportunity to bring up her children and to educate them after such difficult beginnings. We took it for granted that we could go to a grammar school, we even had music lessons. The university was open to us and we all knew that we wanted a university education. The war after all had shown us that everything can be lost except what one has learnt. By the sixties we had grown up. We were normal young West German people, interested in politics and looking to the West. We were stunned and ashamed as we came to know of the full meaning of Hitler's crimes. President Kennedy's 'new frontiers' excited us and pointed the way forward to a better world. His ideas were important to young people like ourselves who had grown up in a state that saw itself as a makeshift arrangement pending unification. West Germany gave us security and a purpose in life, and it had our critical approval although we knew we were living in a state that had not yet found its ultimate expression.

Later, I was able to experience life in the other half of Germany, the GDR, the socialist state. But that was not until 1975, when my diplomat husband was posted to the new permanent mission of the Federal Republic of Germany in East Berlin. This diplomatic outpost was a result of the new *Ostpolitik*, Bonn's policy of adopting a conciliatory approach to Eastern Europe and the Soviet Union. At that time there could hardly have been a more exciting, challenging task for any West German diplomat than to be in East Berlin.

The division of Germany, as it seemed then, could not be overcome within the foreseeable future. It also made no sense to ignore the second German state any longer. And so West Germany decided to make the best of the division and to help the people in the two states to be in touch with each other. The Federal Republic of Germany and the GDR agreed on a 'special relationship', and they set up permanent missions in each other's territories. My husband was a member of the staff in the office in East Berlin and to our delight we were allowed to live right amongst GDR people in Niederschönhausen. This is a leafy

suburb of East Berlin which had escaped war damage, but whose faded pre-war villas had fallen into general neglect.

All our senses told us that the GDR was different from the Germany we knew. In the streets there was the unmistakable smell of the 'Trabis', East Germany's cars. In the cinemas there was disinfectant. There were the grey façades of once beautiful houses; the heaps of lignite, the coal used for domestic heating, stuck on the pavement in front of cellar windows; the dark backyards of the working quarters. There were the huge parade grounds in the city centre, usually empty and with the wind almost permanently howling across them. They filled only for official ceremonies.

Different again were the villages, somehow untouched by the passage of war, caught in an earlier time warp. The storks were still nesting on the roofs, and the neglected beauty of the old traditional German landscape was still in evidence: the fusion of village and fields, unfenced roads, avenues of trees, cobblestones, summer paths and flocks of sheep, the countryside stretching over the horizon. That is how Germany used to look, and it made a strong contrast with the 'modernized' rural landscapes of the West.

It was constantly thrilling for us to live in this other part of Germany, cut off from the West, distant and yet familiar. The GDR gave us the most varied and bewildering sensations – it was a challenge. We were in Germany and yet it was not the Germany we knew. It was our *Heimat* and yet alien. It was close to us and yet remote and unapproachable. It was a curious feeling to stand beside the graves of Schiller and Goethe, or to see Naumburg cathedral. It was part of our German culture and yet we were seemingly treated as foreigners. It was like standing, heart beating fast, in the entrance of your parents' house, knowing that it had passed on to others.

Many people in the GDR approached us nervously and uncertainly, because they saw us as strangers, as West Germans. We had known that the secret police, the 'Stasi', would watch us wherever we went, but we had not anticipated that the East Germans, our 'fellow Germans' would put us on a pedestal, treat us as superior beings, simply because we came from the West. We knew we were privileged as West Germans but the way we were regarded confused us.

We were lucky because soon we were able to establish meaningful contact and have serious discussions with some of our new East German friends.

The village pond at Seifhennersdorf, Saxony, conveys a sense of the traditional German landscape still found around the older villages of former East Germany.

Above Heilingen, in the Hexengrund valley, Thuringia, exemplifies the unspoilt villages of former East Germany, sitting amid its fields and pastures.

Right Sheep grazing near Arnstadt, Thuringia, present another typical aspect of the traditional German landscape still frequently found in former East Germany.

The great interest, the eagerness to talk, the searching questions, the passionate comparison of the two systems, the communist and the free enterprise system, often went on far into the night. There was none of the complacency that success had brought to West Germany. All of a sudden we found that many of our assumptions were being challenged.

But of course we were fortunate. We could enjoy our experiences in the GDR but we always had the security of knowing that we could leave at any time and pass through the Wall back into the West. For our friends it was different. They were shut in as if in a prison, knowing that the first time they might be allowed to see the other side would not come until they were pensioners.

As a German I still look at the new maps with astonishment and almost disbelief. The irrational split that seemed so inalterable for more than four decades has really gone, and what so obviously belonged together can now be together again. Duder-

stadt in the West German region of Lower Saxony and Wernigerode in the East German region of Saxony-Anhalt, to take only one example, are two small towns virtually next door to each other with almost identical half-timbered buildings. Yet a powerfully fortified border, constantly patrolled, separated them for over forty years. Their people lived under two different social systems and all this has made its impact. It is as if they had both aged but in different ways: the *Wessi*, bright, neat, modernized and self assured, the *Ossi* with the quiet dignity of a half-neglected town.

In 1986 the whole of Europe was surveyed to establish its precise geographical centre. Inevitably, it was in Germany: Heilbronn on the Neckar in Baden-Württemberg, which is not far away from Germany's own centre point after unification, at Mihla in Thuringia.

Germany's position at the centre of Europe has shaped its history and is reflected in almost every

Despite the former split between East and West Germany, the similarities between older villages on either side of the divide, such as Wernigerode, Saxony-Anhalt, in the East (above left) and Duderstadt, Lower Saxony, in the West (left), have remained apparent.

The variety of German architecture and decoration can be seen in many different types of building, such as the medieval cloister of the Carmelite church in Bamberg (left); the bell tower of the church of St Maria (below far left) at Frauenchiemsee, Bavaria, with its early structure and seventeenth-century onion dome, framed here by the arches of the Romanesque *Torhalle* (gatehouse); the Renaissance council chamber in Münster town hall (below left); the chancel of St Ägidien, Hülsede, Lower Saxony (above right), with its Renaissance wall memorial and later altarpiece; and the Baroque high altar of the parish church of Landsberg am Lech, Bavaria (far right).

aspect of its life. The other major connected factor that has made the nation what it is today is the variety of external influences it has been subjected to. Both strands are reflected in its landscape, in its climate and in the way its people, its architecture and its culture have developed.

It is easy enough to ignore that Germany only achieved real political unity in the late nineteenth century, when Berlin became the capital of the German Reich. But the new metropolis on the River Spree never quite succeeded in dominating the other old German cities, the residences of the territorial rulers. They had followed different cultural models to that of Berlin and had often allowed foreign influences to predominate. Hamburg, the old harbour and trading city, sometimes seems to be more British than German. Cologne on the banks of the Rhine has a French-inspired Gothic cathedral that has become its great symbol. Dresden, one of the most northerly Baroque cities in Europe, has absorbed more Italian influence than any other German city. But all over Germany in its many towns and cities there is the same architectural mix of foreign and domestic influences.

The enormous variety of landscape, architecture, towns, villages and houses in Germany and the many different regional customs and habits of dress, culture and tradition are far too numerous to be covered in one book. We Germans are now on a journey of mutual rediscovery, and in the process we are defining our new identity as a reunited nation. By revealing something of our common heritage, this book may help us Germans and also some of our friends abroad to understand the ingredients that make up our common culture.

Further examples of German decorative and architectural styles: Rococo stuccowork on the ceiling of the entrance hall of the Church of the Birth of the Virgin in Rottenbuch, Bavaria (above); late Rococo detail from the Ovid Gallery in the Neue Kammern at Sanssouci, Potsdam (left); Neoclassical interior of the Befreiungshalle, or Liberation Hall, at Kelheim, Bavaria (right); Neoclassical interior of the Trinitatiskirche, Cologne (opposite above); and the modern municipal theatre in Münster (opposite below), together with a corner of the remains of the classical-style Romberg Hof.

LANDSCAPE

*Germany's landscape descends like the steps of a huge
stairway from the high mountains in the south, with its
lakes like Weissensee (opposite) in the Bavarian Alps,
through extensive upland areas with villages like
Wagenstieg (above) in the Black Forest, down to the
central and northern plains and finally to the sea.*

Left: Mist rises over Weissensee, near Füssen in Bavaria, revealing the steep pine-clad slopes of the hills to the south.

Right: A Baroque pilgrimage church (built 1733) in a romantic setting at Künterweg near Berchtesgaden, Bavaria.

When I was young I spent several years in Asia. I can still remember my excitement at arriving in the tropics after the mild climate of northern Europe. The vibrant force of the sun was thrilling, and the sharp outlines and short deep shadows made every-thing stand out very vividly. Sometimes, I must admit, I longed for the understatement of the German climate, the sun behind clouds, a grey day, gentle, persistent rain and half-shadows. I missed the contrasts between winter and summer, the morbid browns of autumn and the varied greens of spring. I remembered the twilight and mist, slanting sun rays and the slow transition from day to night.

Calmly the night entered the land,
Leant dreaming against the mountain wall. . . .

The atmosphere in Eduard Mörike's poem is entirely European. The landscapes in Germany are not dramatic, and you do not find strongly contrasting colours next to each other as you do in the tropics, they follow each other as the seasons change.

Nevertheless, it is difficult to say what is most characteristic, for on a closer look Germany is confusingly varied. Perhaps it is easier to say what it is not. I have seen places where nature has so much power and force that one feels like a tiny mite on a

parade ground, small and helpless. Germany cannot offer experience of that kind. It has no deserts and no steppes, no fields of ice or jungles. It is not a country of geographical extremes. As the Berlin writer Alfred Kerr said: 'It is all only magnificent in moderation, no primeval force, no peaks of any kind. But if you know what's good, a moderate summer in Germany is a great and refreshing blessing.'

The big dramas in our landscape were played out long ago. One was the ice age, 600,000 years ago, when gigantic glaciers moved down from the Arctic, depositing a layer of ice many hundred metres thick over the north and west of Germany. They also

Right The remote Hintersee area above Ramsau, Bavaria, in late autumn. There is snow on the mountains before the leaves have fallen in the valley below.

Opposite The pilgrimage church of St Bartholomä, on Königssee in Bavaria, shines like a candle in a darkened room. Its twin Baroque domes are dwarfed by the Watzmann mountains and it is only accessible by boat.

The rich landscape of the Black Forest – the highest part of Germany's *Mittelgebirge*, or secondary range of hills – can contain even a small town like Gengenbach. Vines, like those in the foreground growing on a south-west facing slope, are to be found all over the region.

moved down from the Alps, covering large areas of the south. Their ice masses smoothed the ground beneath them like tissue paper, filling fissures and valleys with boulders and rubble. When the glaciers withdrew, they left their entire cargo of stones and earth masses behind, and streams from the melting ice cut deep rifts in the land. In the north German plain and the Alpine foreland the great upheaval finally created a gentle and appealing moraine landscape of undulating ground or rolling hills, moors, broad lakes and river valleys – the essential German scene.

The other big drama had already taken place in the Tertiary period, 60 million years ago, when immense pressure forced the top layer of the European continent upwards, pressing huge masses against each other. The central area split apart and layers of rock that until then had lain undisturbed, one above the other, now lay askew, broken into blocks and pushed up against each other or down into the depths of the earth. The results were astonishing: the island of Heligoland, for instance, is like a wine-red lump of sandstone tossed into the North Sea, a strange phenomenon in a limestone region. The red stone comes from a geological formation that is only to be found at great depth elsewhere in northern Germany and only reappears on the surface in the highlands of the south. Here the coloured sandstone has provided the building material for some of Germany's finest castles; the world-famous Renaissance castle at Heidelberg is one of them. Heligoland has made its own contribution to Germany's identity. In the north-west corner of the island rises a red sandstone tower known as Tall Anna, and here in 1841, at the top of the cliff, Hoffmann von Fallersleben wrote the hymn to the Germans which, set to music by Haydn, is now the national anthem.

Certainly, since this geological upheaval the physical geography of Germany has been rather disorganized. There does not seem to be any obvious point of reference for the individual regions. No central mountain range, for instance, around which wide plains group, as in France, no backbone of mountains, as in Italy, and no basin surrounded by a ring of mountains, as in Bohemia and Moravia. Germany lies in the centre of Europe like a blunt wedge, stretching from the Alps to the sea, from the Rhine in the west to the Oder in the east. It is interesting that the landscape also underlines the great theme that recurs over and over again in history

and culture, right up to the present: Germany's central position. All the varieties of landscape that Europe has to offer are here, in differing proportions. And most of them, be they plains or moors, rivers or seas, hills or high Alps, continue over the borders of Germany into her neighbouring countries.

All these types of landscape do form a kind of system, however, in that one can progress down from the mountains in the south to the sea in the north as down the steps of a huge stairway. The top stair is of course the high Alps. They are so famous that it is surprising to learn they account for less than 2 per cent of the total ground surface of the country. But they offer all the wildness and romantic nature Jean Jacques Rousseau desired. 'I know', he said in *Confessions*, 'what I regard as a fine district. Never a plain, however beautiful it may be. I want rushing streams, rocks, firs, dark forests, mountains, paths which lead steeply up and down and a fearful ravine beside my way.' More gently, but with equal emphasis, Königssee in Bavaria reveals the power of the mountains. Its water is so blue that it looks as if it goes down as far as the huge walls of rock tower above it. Where the lake and the mountain masses meet stands the round white church of St Bartholomä, the only detail created by the hand of man.

Wild, romantic scenery like that admired by Rousseau can also be found on the next stage of our journey to the sea, in the secondary chain of mountains or hills known as the *Mittelgebirge*. They stretch in a broad band, starting in the south-east with the Bavarian Forest. Their northern edge curves from Aachen across the Harz to Dresden on the Elbe with a varied patchwork of landscapes between. The highest part of these hills is in the Black Forest in the south-west of Germany. Is it really darker than all the other German forests, or does it only seem so because of its name? Certainly, the higher one climbs, the darker the trunks of the trees appear. They are blackish brown against the green of the fir trees. Involuntarily, I think of the medieval fear of the forest and I remember Albrecht Altdorfer's small picture showing St George, bent and tiny on his horse, before a kind of German jungle, an amorphous, all-engulfing mass of pitch black trees and bushes. One wooded ravine in the Black Forest is actually called 'Cry for Help'.

Hesse and Thuringia are related landscapes in many respects. In the period when Germany was territorially fragmented they were politically closer

Left A patchwork of small irregularly shaped fields, put to a variety of uses, is a typical sight in the northern part of the Black Forest, as here between Lahr and Zell.

A watermill with twin wheels near Furtwangen-Neukirch in the Black Forest. Constructed in 1825, it has been used since 1839 by one family to power their clockmaking business.

than other neighbouring states, and it was particularly irrational that the latest internal German
border, the Iron Curtain, separated these two areas.
Reunification has released Thuringia from its unfortunate position as a border state, and it can now
rightly be called the 'green heart of Germany' again,
with its wealth of forests and fertile fields on rich,
loess soil. The River Saale, which winds in picturesque curves and bends through the Thuringian
hills, was the eastern border of the Holy Roman
Empire for a long time in the Middle Ages. A
broad, dark, wooded area, the Thuringian Forest,
stretches down to the Franconian Forest, and firs
and pines have now replaced the eighteenth-
century beechwoods.

The hills of Hesse are also richly forested. Gladed
beechwoods grow on sandstone or limestone soil, and
between their silvery-grey trunks blueberries are to
be found in summer and mushrooms in autumn.
This is where the Brothers Grimm collected fairy
stories at the beginning of the nineteenth century,
going from village to village and faithfully recording
the tales that had been handed down orally from one
generation to the next. In this region many villages
still seem so untouched that you feel that Hansel and
Gretel could still be wandering in the surrounding
woods. In Erlangen, further south, Ludwig Tieck
and his friend Wackenroder met in 1793 to start on
their walk through the Main-Franconian area. This
turned out to be a major turning-point in German
literary and intellectual life, for Tieck and Wackenroder were so enraptured by the beauty of the region
that in 1798 Tieck wrote an intense and emotional
account of the journey in the form of a novel called
Franz Sternbalds Wanderungen, which influenced
the rise of the Romantic movement in Germany.

However, it would be a distortion to describe only
the timeless and idyllic aspects of the German
landscape. The nineteenth and twentieth centuries
have brought more changes to the face of the country
than all the centuries before. Where the range of hills
gives way to the north German plain lie many of the
big industrial areas which account for much of
Germany's present standing in the world. The
slightly hilly area between the River Lippe and the
River Ruhr is now one of the most densely populated
parts of Germany and one of the biggest urban
landscapes in Europe. The Ruhr industrial belt is
built on coal, and with the steelworks of Krupp and
Thyssen it became the industrial heart of Europe in

Above Two views of the Kahla valley in Thuringia, the 'green heart of Germany'. Leuchtenberg castle (left), a medieval stronghold, stands at the head of the valley. This predominantly agricultural region in the south-east has escaped both neglect and overdevelopment.

Left Soft light and colours often prevail in the Saale valley in eastern Thuringia.

Right Villages like Unterregenbach in north Bavaria are still fully integrated into the landscape and traditional way of life.

the nineteenth century. Slag heaps, pits, winding towers, long rows of one- and two-storeyed miners' dwellings are characteristic of this nineteenth-century industrial zone.

The economic face of the twentieth century is different. Not many landscapes in Germany have changed so much since 1945 as the Rhine plain on either side of the autobahn between Cologne and Bonn. Near Cologne, for instance, an extensive and elegant residential quarter has grown up since the war. It is the Hahnwald, where the leading figures from local business and industry have built their prestigious villas. Not far away a massive industrial complex has evolved over the last forty years. Here the sky is often cloudy, and few people are to be seen; the huge mass of interweaving pipes makes the refineries look like a disembowelled, primeval metal creature by day, while by night the cold neon lights strengthen this science fiction impression of a structure from outer space.

Saxony, at the eastern end of Germany's *Mittelgebirge*, contains some of the most interesting and attractive landscapes of former East Germany, such as the area known as Saxon Switzerland (left above), south-east of Dresden. These strange rock formations were created by the movement of water in prehistoric times, when the level of the nearby River Elbe was much higher. In the Zittauer Gebirge, a region of gently undulating hills in south-east Saxony, there are remote rural areas like this deserted valley near Lückendorf (opposite), almost on the Czechoslovakian border, as well as traditional half-timbered farmhouses like that at Jonsdorf (left below).

Two aspects of the north German plains near Lüchow, Lower Saxony: the heathland of Nemitzer Heide (above), carpeted with purple heather in August, and the small town of Schnackenburg (right) on a bend of the River Elbe, which is much frequented by small pleasure boats as well as larger craft.

Above and right The plains of northern Germany also contain expanses of forest like that near Feldberg (above) in Mecklenburg-Western Pomerania, while the river scene just after sunset near Neubrandenburg (right) illustrates the abundance of water in this part of Germany with all its lakes and rivers.

In the west and the north the range of hills gives way to the plains of the Lower Rhine, Lower Saxony and Mecklenburg, and the last great stage begins as we move towards the sea. Again we find a different kind of variety: wide, flat land in Westphalia, rich pastures in Lower Saxony and Schleswig-Holstein, fertile fruit farms in the Altes Land near Hamburg, then moorland with old and dilapidated farms, dark marshland with prosperous, well-kept buildings, followed by the thinner, sandy 'Geest' soil and in the east the Mecklenburg lakes.

In the far north lies the last and lowest stage, the sea; in fact, Germany is fortunate to have two coastlines. The North Sea is wild, rough and open, on the edge of the Atlantic. The borders between the green-grey sea and the land are blurred, for as the tide rises and falls it creates wide mud flats with a grey and sometimes blue-black coating. Nowhere is the smell of the sea as pungent as here. The North Sea is pressing south, and over time it has eaten away large sections of the flat, north German coast land. The inhabitants of this region have taken refuge from the floods that have constantly attacked their homes by building houses on artificial mounds of earth. The great achievement of the Frisians on the North Sea coast was to construct large dykes to give protection from the ceaseless battering of the waves. All adults had to do their share of the work on the dykes, and this community effort helped to level social differences.

The Baltic is milder and more appealing. It has beautiful sandy beaches, with blue and green waters. The old, abandoned resorts still display remnants of the glamour and elegance with which they attracted the noble and wealthy in the last century, although they are on the brink of finally disappearing, or being renovated and changed altogether.

Only the white chalk cliffs on Rügen, an island just off the Baltic coast, are above the currents of fashion. Perhaps they are actually doing what Oscar Wilde said nature as a whole did: copying art. For since they were painted by Caspar David Friedrich, it is difficult not to see them through the artist's eyes. The gaping white rocks frame the endless expanse of the sea, and we look into its depths as if the world had only just been created and the earth were visibly rounding on the horizon before our very eyes.

Water is a major element in the German landscape, and it too is largely a consequence of the country's central position. The climate depends as

Left and right Rügen, lying off the Baltic coast, is the largest of Germany's offshore islands. The strange limestone rock formations (left) rising from the sea near Sassnitz are known as the Wissower Klinken and are probably part of an open crack or fissure formed in an early ice age. Thatched cottages are still common on the island, like this priest's widow's house at Gross Zicker (right).

Below One of the numerous lakes of north-east Germany: Brückentinsee near Feldberg, Mecklenburg-Western Pomerania.

much on the oceanic weather from the Atlantic, which affects the British Isles and the French channel coast, as on the continental air flows and temperature variations from the east and the vastness of Asia. This central position gives Germany an average temperature of 9° C (48° F) and a moist, changeable climate.

There is indeed no lack of rain. In the writings of Tacitus, the Roman historian, who was the first to record the ethnology of 'Germania', you can sense the shock he felt coming from the sun of Italy to the unwelcoming climate north of the Alps. Germania was dreadful because of its forests, he said, writing about a hundred years after the birth of Christ, ugly because of its bogs, the sky was generally cloudy and the earth shrouded in rain or dripping mist. Today we need to look after our bogs and moors and we fear for the survival of the German forests. But water is still flowing as freely, and green – the green of vegetation – is still the dominant colour of these landscapes from above. Only where the mountains are too high or the area too densely populated is green not predominant.

A welcome consequence of the moist climate is the number of lakes. The largest and most southerly is Lake Constance, and it is actually no more than a widening of the Rhine as it leaves its deeply incised bed and spreads over flooded meadows. The lake stretches west to the wooded slopes of the Black Forest, and the villages, monastery towers, orchards and vineyards on its banks have become an intrinsic part of this landscape and of traditional south German culture.

How different are the Brandenburg lakes in the east. Here one can tell that the drainage of the wet areas around the River Oder and in the marshy Spreewald only began a short time ago, in the eighteenth century. Until then this core area of Prussia, with its striking combination of pine forests, sand and bogs, was at least a century behind the west German territories in development terms. The 'Soldier King', the father of Frederick the Great, was the first to try and tackle this major task. His son Frederick wrote during the Seven Years' War: 'It is not necessary for me to survive; but it is necessary for me to do my duty.' When his long wars were over he made it his duty to drain the great marshlands in his state, and when Frederick died, in 1786, he had created 1000 new villages and 60,000 settlements for 360,000 people.

Two lakes near Füssen, Bavaria: Alpsee (opposite) and Weissensee (right), with the church spire of Weissensee village. Like many of the smaller, lesser-known Bavarian lakes, their shores are sparsely populated and the waters frequented mainly by local fishermen.

The waters that wind as rivers through the plains or lie as lakes in the valleys and depressions of the old moraines work together with the light, infertile soil to produce an adequate base for the pine forests, so creating the particular charm of this Prussian landscape. On its eastern edge flows the River Oder, and it now forms the border between Germany and Poland; the river flows through a broad primeval valley past the border lowlands and the Mecklenburg plain with its lakes. Another major river is the Havel, the 'cradle of Prussia', as the real discoverer of this area, the novelist Theodor Fontane, called it. On its banks the Prussians once defeated the ancient inhabitants of the area between the Elbe and the Oder, the Wendts. The Great Elector also defeated the Swedes here in 1675, although they had hoped to remain with their armies in Germany long after the Thirty Years' War ended in 1648. The Havel flows, with many twists and bends, and past many romantic lakes from the Mecklenburg plains to the Elbe.

The River Spree winds through the same region; it rises in Oberlausitz in Saxony and makes its way, with innumerable bends, through forests of alder and oak, to Berlin, where it joins the Havel. In the Spree region the rowing boat is still the most frequent means of transport, to bring in the harvest or reach the next town. Fontane commented in a poem:

> So that these winding water tracks
> The charm of Venice do not lack
> The countless streams are traversed here
> By the boat of the Spreewald gondolier.

Perhaps it is rather ambitious to compare this region with Venice. Nevertheless, it does have an unmistakeable charm, with its countless lakes and waterways in a flat or slightly rolling landscape. It offers something for every taste, with lakes large and small, marshy or reeded, sandy or forested, remote or populated, desolate or charming. You hope and fear at once that its quiet beauty will soon be discovered by more people.

The great rivers of Germany have long been famous, most of all the Rhine. It does in fact have something unusual to offer: from Bingen to Bonn alone there are fifty castles, an average of one castle every 2 kilometres ($1\frac{1}{4}$ miles), so that from each castle you can see the battlements of the next. This makes the Middle Rhine the area with the most castles in the world. It is hard to resist the impression made by the narrow Rhine gorge, which bears the ruins of its castles as proudly as scars, telling of the battles and legends of the Middle Ages. There have certainly been battles here, but they were not as romantic as we like to imagine. In the castles above the Rhine sat the robber barons; they controlled transport on the river and exacted dues to force on the goods that were taken on the old trade route from south to north.

Of particular importance in discovering the romance of the Rhine were the educational journeys made by the British nobility in the seventeenth and eighteenth centuries, on their Grand Tour to the southern courts of Europe. Later came Lord Byron, praising the Middle Rhine landscape in *Childe Harold's Pilgrimage*. Before him, at the beginning of the nineteenth century, the Germans had also discovered their river, and since the Romantic movement the rocky landscapes had no longer been seen as rude and repellent but as unspoilt and beautiful. The old castles were considered major works of art, testimonies to German history and to a national identity.

In fact the Rhine does embody a complex of

Königstein, Saxony, stands on one of Germany's great rivers, the Elbe, overlooked by the castle hill in the background. The town has a strong musical tradition and was the birthplace of several composers.

qualities and developments crucial in German history, if not as it appeared to the Romantics. It has become the quintessential German river, although it neither rises in Germany nor enters the sea within her borders. The Germans' insistent search for themselves and their national identity began, understandably and justifiably at the time, in the Wars of Liberation against Napoleon. Then in the 1830s a minor poet, Nikolaus Becker, wrote a successful poem, 'Do not let them have it, the free German Rhine', meaning the French. The Rhine was no longer an invitation to bridge-building; it became a border on which nationalism kept watch. After the Franco-Prussian War of 1870–71 it finally became an element in German patriotism and was adorned with pompous national monuments. Today, after the major tragedies of two world wars, the Rhineland has regained its function of linking peoples, and can resume its two-thousand-year tradition as a landscape for cultural interchange.

Far left The Elbe from Bastei Rock, which rises 194 metres (637 ft) above the river in the Saxon Switzerland area.

Below left Füssen overlooks the River Lech in Bavaria. Towns on rivers, often dominated by castles, are commonly found throughout Germany and especially in the south.

Left The Havel river, in an almost rural setting only 12 miles (19 km) to the north-west of Berlin city centre.

Below Pfalzgrafenstein castle sits on an island in the Rhine opposite Kaub in Rhineland-Palatinate. It was built as a collecting point for Rhine tolls. In 1327 when the central toll tower was built, there was only one shipping lane, to the east, which could if necessary be blocked.

ARCHITECTURE

*German architecture has been influenced by many foreign
ideas, but a uniquely German style has often evolved from
these influences, as can be seen in the Rococo monastery
library at Wiblingen (opposite) and the Romanesque
carving in St Michael's Church, Hildesheim (above).*

THE MIDDLE AGES

The history of Germany as an identifiable region is often dated to AD 9, when Arminius, the ruler of a Germanic tribe, defeated the Romans, who withdrew back over the Rhine. However, it was not until the establishment of the Frankish kingdom of Charlemagne that the area achieved any political cohesion. Charlemagne succeeded in building up a realm that stretched from the Elbe to the Pyrenees, and so both the French and the Germans rightly regard him as one of their kings. The kingdom of the Franks ended the confusion of the great migrations that had shaken the continent of Europe in the first 800 years after the birth of Christ. The word *deutsch* (German) probably first came into use during the Frankish period and initially referred only to the language spoken in the eastern part of the realm, although it eventually came to apply to the region, *Deutschland*, which German speakers lived in.

It was evident, however, even in Charlemagne's time that Roman culture was not dead, and in later centuries, too, hardly a generation or style of art could deny its debt to antiquity. The pope and the emperor, the two poles of power in the Middle Ages, each took up the traditions of the old Roman empire for their own reasons. They felt jointly called upon to rule the Western world, and art was pressed into their service as well. Life for people in the Middle Ages was governed by faith in the revelations of the Bible. Each work of art was a part of that firmly fixed system and was intended to provide an image of it. Throughout the Middle Ages, therefore, the major architectural works were commissioned by the church; it was the cradle and centre of cultural life.

In the 'Carolingian Renaissance' Roman and Byzantine, Christian and Frankish culture met. Aachen is an impressive testimony to the combining of older traditions with the creativity of the Franks. This is where Charlemagne had his imperial seat, the *Pfalz*, or Palatinate. In 792 a chapel was added and today it is surrounded by a Gothic minster. The chapel is so well preserved that the ideas expressed in its structure are still clearly evident.

The chapel in Aachen is a two-storey, octagonal, centralized structure on a ground plan of Byzantine origin. The court church of the Roman emperors in Ravenna, the city that was once the centre of Byzantine culture in the western world, served as a

Left The west end, or 'westwork' (873–85), of the former monastery church at Corvey, near Höxter in North Rhine-Westphalia. It was built for the use of the German emperors when they attended the monks' divine services.

Right The entrance portal and part of the nave of the massive three-aisled Romanesque basilica of Paulinzella, near Rudolstadt in Thuringia. Built in the early twelfth century during a period of ecclesiastical reform stemming from Cluny, it was named after the original abbess, Paulina, a Saxon noblewoman who supervised the construction herself.

Far right The entrance hall of the Romanesque convent church (1140–50) at Lippoldsberg, Hesse, on the Weser, bears a curious resemblance to a crypt. Some of the capitals are decorated with fine leaf and scale motifs.

Right: The early-thirteenth-century cloister of St Peter and St Johannes in Berchtesgaden, Bavaria. Much of the church was Gothicized later, but this Romanesque cloister has survived in unusually fine condition.

model, and the design was also influenced by the Lateran palace in Rome. Charlemagne regarded it as so important to be seen as successor to the Roman emperors that he had antique columns dismantled in Ravenna and Rome and transported to Aachen across the Alps. Since then they have adorned the arched openings in the triforium from which the Emperor once looked down into his church.

The 'westwork' of the chapel, on the other hand, with its two doors behind the emperor's throne, is a Frankish creation. It is a multi-storeyed building to the west of the chapel, closed to the outside like a castle and opening to the inside; from the raised imperial box you can see the altars inside the church. It would be hard to imagine a more powerful architectural symbol for the unity of church and state. The westwork became a leitmotif in German Romanesque architecture and it is repeated in many later churches. Charlemagne's Palatine chapel became the symbolic centrepiece of the Carolingian kingdom and later the church where German emperors and kings were crowned.

Left The Jewish baths in Speyer, Rhineland-Palatinate, date from 1110–20 and are believed to be the work of the builders responsible for Speyer cathedral. This may explain their rather monumental (though small-scale) design. The dimly lit subterranean rooms have barrel and groin vaulting and were used by Jewish women for ritual cleansing purposes.

Opposite The ground level arcade in the two-storey cloister of the cathedral at Hildesheim, Lower Saxony. The massively thick walls and squat, rounded vaulting are typically Romanesque, but the presence of an upper storey is unusual for the period.

Below Detail from a capital in the St Peter and St Johannes cloister, Berchtesgaden, showing a half human head on a lion's body.

Romanesque, the first pan-European art style after the decline of the Roman empire, developed from the Carolingian Renaissance. The very name, 'Romanesque', shows how much it owes to Rome and antiquity, but the essential characteristics of the young Germanic peoples in the eastern part of the Carolingian empire, who were just entering world history, also found artistic expression in this style. The controlled monumentality and the simple, severe forms of architecture that is earthbound with its massive walls but looking to heaven in spirit are considered to be typically Germanic. The Romanesque period only reached its peak around the year 1000, after the huge empire of Charlemagne had collapsed into a west Frankish and an east Frankish kingdom. In the eastern part, from which the Holy Roman Empire was later to develop, three mighty Saxon emperors, the Ottonians, ruled in the tenth century. They brought their lands great prosperity, and wonderful early Romanesque buildings were

The nave of St Michael's Church, Hildesheim (1007–33) – a three-aisled basilica with a painted wooden ceiling – is lit by high clerestory windows, and its walls are supported by an arcade of double columns alternating with a single pier.

Right The angel choir screen at St Michael's Church, Hildesheim, dates from the late twelfth century. This south side is decorated with sitting angels and (below) a frieze of fantastical creatures.

Far right This capital on the south side of St Michael's nave also illustrates the late Romanesque style of carving. It has recently been restored, and the red and white colour scheme of the arches above is supposed to imitate the original.

Right below Thirteenth-century stone bust of Bishop Bernward, the founder of St Michael's, who flourished around the turn of the millenium. The worn, pitted appearance of the bust, as if it had been savagely attacked at some stage, somehow lends greater strength to this portrayal of one of the most powerful ecclesiastical princes of his time.

erected under their rule. In the following Salian and Staufen dynasties German Romanesque reached its peak, while in the western Frankish lands, which are now France, the Gothic style was already developing.

On a hill above the city of Hildesheim in Lower Saxony a three-aisled basilica with double transepts, double choir and many towers has survived for nearly a thousand years – a mighty monument to God on earth. The church of St Michael is an early Romanesque structure (built 1007–33) and has all the majestic beauty of that style. Its walls and towers are heavy and dignified; huge masses of stone are grouped and graded. The ground plan is in the shape of the Holy Cross and its harmonious proportions are based on the dimensions of the square formed by the crossing of the nave and transepts.

St Michael has typically Romanesque elements, such as the triple rhythm of two columns and one pier along the arcades separating the nave from the aisles. It creates an impression of calm but dynamic force, with spaces given both horizontal and vertical emphasis. Each internal area is visually integrated into the whole and at the same time clearly distinguished from the neighbouring space. Apart from the westwork, another typical feature of German Romanesque found at Hildesheim is to have the main entrance to the church on the south side and not, as in France, for instance, in the west front.

On all Romanesque buildings arches dominate, and they lend the architecture its particular weight and majesty. They are pure semicircles, and derive from the round arches and arcades of antiquity. The Germanic builders were well familiar with these arches; they had seen them on their journeys to Rome and they also knew them from the many Roman remains in their own lands, like aqueducts and the Porta Nigra in Trier. In Romanesque churches the arch is both a support and an ornamentation. In the nave arches link the pillars and piers that carry the dividing walls, and mighty triumphal arches separate nave, aisles and choir. The arch also lends rhythm and harmony to the triforium and clerestory and it structures the outside walls. Later, in the high Romanesque period, the outside walls

Left Carved sculpture on capitals, often depicting a strange world of demons and distorted faces, is very much a feature of the Romanesque period. This example comes from the cloister of St Peter and St Johannes in Berchtesgaden, Bavaria.

Right The east end of St Aposteln, Cologne (1192–1240). This imposing configuration of apse, transepts and towers is often seen in German Romanesque churches, especially those in Cologne.

were punctured and enlivened with small galleries. Their Italian arcade style was due to the dynastic link between Lombardy in Upper Italy and the Holy Roman Empire. The arch at the entrance to the late Romanesque church of St Andreas in Cologne is powerful and expressive in its simplicity, its use of repetition and its shift of perspective, as it leads into the mysterious solemnity of the holy building.

The cubic shape of the capitals in many early Romanesque churches is as simple and strong as the round arch. Block capitals form a cushion between the rising column and the downward thrust of the walls they support. The column rises high into the square at its top, as if the round and cube were interpenetrating. The simple, solid shape fits the monumental character of the Romanesque churches and it emphasizes the powerful uniformity of the interior. The smooth sides were probably once painted, like the walls of the church itself. Some of the capitals are also decorated with stone leaves and palmettes. As the Romanesque period developed, the carved ornamentation and sculptures on the capitals became more elaborate, revealing a strange aspect of the medieval world: distorted visages with plants and dragons emerging from their mouths, demons, lions, women with fish tails, birds, snakes and other creatures, as if a turbulent world of spirits were waiting to be released from these small stone prisons.

The vaulting in Romanesque churches is probably what impresses us most today. The Romanesque period did not invent this, it revived it and imbued it with Christian symbolism. St Michael in Hildesheim still has a flat, painted wooden roof over its nave, but in the crypt, cloisters and smaller adjacent areas vaulting is already in use; in later Romanesque

Left The cathedral of Limburg an der Lahn, Hesse, was completed in about 1250, following earlier French and German models, including St Gevern in Cologne. The coloured decoration, restored in 1968–72, is based on the remains of thirteenth-century plaster discovered there.

Above The east end of the *Münster*, or cathedral, at Essen in North Rhine-Westphalia, built between the eleventh and fourteenth centuries and restored in 1951–9 after sustaining damage in the Second World War. The Romanesque columns and arches are surmounted by Gothic vaulting.

Right The (restored) entrance to the crypt in the late Romanesque church of St Andreas, Cologne.

churches it was to determine the overall artistic effect. The cathedral at Speyer was the first great vaulted structure of the West in the Middle Ages. It was already a masterpiece of classical Roman monumentality, softened by the gentle warmth of its red sandstone, when it still had its flat wooden roof. In the twelfth century Heinrich IV, the most ambitious of the Staufen emperors, ordered the huge nave to be raised by a groin vault, for such a vault would create a greater space. 'This noble structure was erected by our forebears Konrad and Heinrich and Ourselves,' proclaimed the emperor when it was finished, the first groin-vaulted basilica in the Western world. It was a proud demonstration of imperial might at a time when a cathedral in Cluny, the centre of the religious revival, was being built with a severe, simple barrel vault. The spatial impact of Speyer cathedral is still overwhelming. So is its symbolic

Right The interior of Limburg cathedral. Although the cathedral is basically late Romanesque, there are numerous signs of the new Gothic style, including peaked arches and leaf capitals.

Left Part of the ruined Eldena monastery at Greifswald in Mecklenburg-Western Pommerania. Of medieval origin, it attracted the attention of the romantic painter Caspar David Friedrich in the nineteenth century, who depicted it in many works.

Below The west end of the massive Romano-Gothic cathedral of St Paul (1172–1265) in Münster. The twin towers are Romanesque, the remainder early Gothic.

significance, for the emperor wanted to erect an earthly image of the celestial vaults of heaven.

In France a new style had developed as early as the twelfth century, but Germany adopted it only slowly. It was Gothic. How closely the Germans clung to Romanesque, perhaps the most 'Germanic' of all the styles in their architectural history, is evident from the hesitancy to use the new way of building east of the Rhine. Speyer cathedral had still aimed to capture the cosmos in great blocks of stone laid one on top of the next and hold it firmly on the ground. The Gothic idea of space was quite different. Now builders wanted to release the church from its earthbound links and allow it to stretch upwards and reach the sky physically and spiritually. Demons vanished from its interior and turned into gargoyles sitting on the roof ridge outside, spewing the dark

Right Red brick became fashionable in north Germany in the late Gothic period and was used here at the Wienhausen nunnery, near Celle in Lower Saxony. With their stepped gables and blind Gothic arches, the façades of the nun's church (right) and the west wing of the nunnery are good examples of the *Backsteingotik* (Brick Gothic) style.

The defensive walls of Burg Trausnitz, above Landshut. The city's name means 'protector of the region' and it preceded Munich as the capital of Bavaria. The castle itself, founded in 1204, was the original core of the city. These walls and towers were added in the late Gothic period, with characteristic use of red brick.

Left Interior of the parish church of St George (1488–99) in Dinkelsbühl, Bavaria. It is one of the best examples of Germany's late Gothic hall churches, where the aisles are the same height as the nave. The ceiling, with its net-vaulting, is supported by slender clusters of columns, like trees reaching skywards in a forest.

Right The north aisle of the cathedral in Brunswick, Lower Saxony. The original Romanesque single aisle was replaced in the late fifteenth century by this unusual two-aisled hall, with twisted columns and elaborate vaulting.

Far right Fifteenth-century relief carving above one of the doors (known as the Bride's Gate) to St Martin's Church in Landshut, Bavaria, depicting a circumcision.

rainwater away from the church wall, or they became creatures crawling beneath the feet of the saints, as if the dark, mysterious threat that had appeared on the Romanesque pillars and arches had become a burlesque.

The structural and technical developments that made these architectural changes possible revolutionized building technique although the individual elements were not altogether new. The main problem for all Romanesque and Gothic churches was to

create supports that would hold the roof. The Romanesque builders had achieved stability with huge thick walls; the Gothic builders created it by balancing and concentrating the forces in the framework of the building. Basically, in doing so they combined two old inventions – the pointed arch in the interior and the buttress on the exterior. The pointed arch, which could be constructed more, or less, steeply, as desired, freed the ground plan from its link with the Roman square.

In length, height and breadth the Gothic building seemed to have no limits, and the size went on increasing, up to the outsize hall churches of the late period. Outside, the church wall was supported at crucial points by buttresses and flying buttresses, which took the sideways and downward thrust of the roof. These additions to the church wall must have seemed absolutely revolutionary. The structural skeleton of the building, with its buttresses and flying buttresses, was no longer hidden under smooth walls, it was visible. The buttresses even form part of the artistic impression, they strive, sway

and tremble upwards, raised ever higher by towers and finials, as if wanting to storm heaven itself with their electric energies.

Clearly, so great an achievement could not be taken further. The immense social effort required for such buildings made them vulnerable to any deterioration in the general situation, like the Black Death and the Hundred Years' War in the fourteenth and fifteenth centuries. A change in attitude brought about by the start of a new age also caused building on Gothic cathedrals to slow down and gradually come to a halt. For these reasons the cathedral in Cologne remained uncompleted for 500 years, until the romantic revival in the nineteenth century rekindled enthusiasm for the 'German style', as Gothic was then called, and completing the cathedral became a national task, which was finally achieved with its consecration in 1880.

Left Two views of the courtyard of Pfalzgrafenstein castle, on an island in the Rhine opposite Kaub, Rhineland-Palatinate. The three-storey defensive wall and courtyard was built in late Gothic times and surrounds the castle's earlier tower.

Above right Late Gothic arcade attached to the Heimathaus in Wasserburg am Inn, Bavaria. Originally, perhaps, the whole overhead area would have been painted in colours similar to those seen in the foreground.

Right Gothic vaulting on the first-floor landing of the town hall (1457–9) at Wasserburg.

Left The barrel-vaulted *Gerichtslaube* (law court) in the town hall at Lüneburg, Lower Saxony, was originally the council chamber. Later it was used for judicial purposes, and the benches, with their Renaissance-style ornamentation, were added in the sixteenth century to accommodate the jury. The ceiling paintings also date from this period.

The kitchen (which dates from the late Gothic period) of Schloss Burgk near Schleiz, Thuringia, and a staircase leading off it (above).

THE RENAISSANCE

All over Europe in the fourteenth and fifteenth centuries the late Gothic movement was showing signs of overload, even exhaustion, and further creative development seemed impossible. This time has been called the autumn of the Middle Ages. Germany took a rather different direction, channelling its creative energies for its cathedrals and minsters into a special 'German Gothic' style. The nave and aisles melted into a huge transparent hall, the vaulted roof grew and was covered with abstract linear compartments. The pillars lost their subdivisions into base, shaft and capital and extended, without stages, ever higher, so that the church roof stood as if on stilts. In these high halls the individual was lost; he was only one of the flock before God, not an individual with a physical existence.

At this point the new movement of the Renaissance, which had already started in Italy in the fourteenth century, took a decisive direction. Man became the scale for all things. Architecture fell back on the strict and noble forms of antique Classical temples, basing the design of columns and pilasters, arches and vaults on sizes and proportions that are immediately understandable to the human eye. The pointed arch gave way to the round arch, and the late Gothic pillar was replaced by the Classical column, while the many-ribbed vault became a barrel vault or a coffered ceiling. On the exterior the portal and shallow pediment created an antique façade. The artists of the Renaissance discovered the measurements of the 'Golden Section' in the ideal human body, and they used this principle to give their works harmony and balance. They discovered how to depict space through perspective and proclaimed new themes – not only to illustrate the stories from the Bible but to show the beauty of life on earth as well. No longer would the purity of spiritual life be all that counted, the perfection of the human form and the individuality of people would matter as well.

The new ideas spread throughout Europe, and many contemporaries celebrated the end of the 'dark Middle Ages'. In every field men aimed to free themselves of the doctrinal authority of the church. The world was to be grasped with the powers of human understanding and the individual personality was to be free to develop. The way was already being prepared for the reformers and Protestants of the

Opposite The interior of the castle chapel at Celle, Lower Saxony, was originally built in Gothic style in 1485 but was remodelled in 1565–70 after the Reformation.

Right The Princes' Gallery (1624) in the chapel of Schloss Burgk near Schleiz, Thuringia, is surmounted by strange, almost primitive, busts of crowned queens.

Below The remarkable ceiling paintings (1577) in the church of St Ägidien at Hülsede, Lower Saxony, represent scenes from the life of Jesus.

next generation. But around 1500, when the Renaissance was already moving towards its peak in Italy, Germany still looked very medieval. Most of the houses had wooden façades. Projecting bays and balconies overshadowed the streets, which were rarely paved, while pointed roofs with Gothic gables completed the scene.

But in comparison with the rest of Europe the standard of living in the cities and palaces was high. Many houses had broad stairways with fixed railings, coloured glass windows and papered or wood-panelled walls. They were already reflecting the great change in the quality of life and in taste which had come from the expansion of trade and commerce and the development of an urban culture. Dürer, Cranach and Holbein painted powerfully built men with broad chests and thick beards who look healthy and robust. In political and social life, however, the forces were not so well balanced. There was tension between the nobility and the peasants; many of the medieval knights had degenerated into robber barons; secular and ecclesiastical princes rivalled each other in a selfish lust for power and wealth; and the papal court was wasteful and open to bribery. Nevertheless, trade and commerce flourished in the cities, and at the universities a new, humanist, younger generation was emerging. In Mainz Gutenberg developed book printing with movable letters.

In this general climate of innovation a German province, Saxony, produced the Reformation and unleashed a tempest that tore the medieval systems apart. Until then people in the Western world had been held together by a common church and its head, the pope. When Martin Luther nailed his 95 theses to the door of the cathedral in Wittenberg on 31 October 1517, he denied the pope his role as Christ's representative on earth, demanding that faith be based solely on the Bible and so sparking off the great attack on Rome. The new truth could be printed overnight now that printing had been invented, and it spread rapidly throughout Germany. A new world church had been born.

The Reformation found open doors all over Germany. Where it met organized resistance, blood flowed in streams. For a short time the religious strife also mingled with the social unrest of the peasants. The conflicts over this religious split were greater than any that had shaken the continent since the conquest of Rome by the barbarians, and the Germans were most affected by the subsequent wars,

A detail from (above) and a section of (right) the upper gallery of the castle chapel at Neuburg an der Donau in Bavaria. The wall and ceiling paintings (1543) depict scenes from the Old and New Testaments.

Above and above right The red brick gables of north Germany: the main square (Am Sande) in Lüneburg is lined with town houses from the Renaissance and other periods. The twisting brick effects and the blind arcades, offset in white, are typical of the region.

the political and social confusion and the theological fanaticism of the age. They were at the epicentre, and they also revealed an unfortunate tendency to be intolerant and inflexible in their convictions, which prevented compromise.

Art in Germany suffered severely under all these struggles. Three of the greatest German artists of the sixteenth century fell victim to the peasants' uprising in southern Germany in 1524–5 because they sympathized with the social suffering of the lower classes: Matthias Neithardt Grünewald had to give up his post at court, and he died soon after, impoverished and neglected; Tilman Riemenschneider was arrested and dishonoured; the least known of them, the painter Jerg Ratgeb, was taken prisoner and quartered.

Of even more consequence was the hostility of Protestantism to the visual arts. Luther insisted that the gospel should not be proclaimed through art but only by the word, accompanied by music, when required. This was because the Bible, printed in German, was now more accessible to people, and the mediation of a priest or the visual arts was no longer necessary. As Will Durand wrote in *The Story of Civilization* (pub. Simon and Schuster, New York, 1963), church architecture hid its head during the

Reformation. Many churches remained unfinished and many, like the Gothic monastery of Eldena near Greifswald, were quarried to provide stone for secular buildings. The few Protestant churches built during these years were demonstratively simple and severe: they were dedicated to a faith that was to be nourished by prayer and the Bible and not by art. Moreover, the Protestants disliked the Renaissance roots in antiquity, a heathen time. They found the basic form of Gothic churches more appropriate, and this explains the strange discrepancy in a religious and intellectual movement that was able to change the ideological face of Europe but could not develop compelling architectural ideas of its own. It created a new church with a community of millions, but not a significant church architecture to express the new faith.

However, the fragmentation of Germany into many smaller states prevented excessive uniformity and softened the severity of the Protestant faith. The small church in Hülsede near Hanover illustrates the epochs of German art history like the rings of a tree. Under its floor a chiselled, grimacing Romanesque head was found a few years ago; at the same time, early Gothic wall paintings were revealed in the vestry, hidden under layers of paint. An unusual

feature are the frescoes decorating the cross vault and the walls of the little church. Following the Religious Peace of Augsburg the community had to adopt the religion of its ruler, and in 1558 the parish of Hülsede became Protestant. Nevertheless the church was decorated, hardly a generation later, with frescoes that cover much of the interior of the church and illustrate traditional Biblical themes.

The Catholic churches from the second half of the sixteenth century are like a demonstration against Protestant severity. They naturally look to the Italian Renaissance, for Italy was the home of their church. The court church of St Michael in Munich is a good example of this, and it is perhaps the most entrancing Italian Renaissance church building on German soil. It was built in the spirit of the religious revival by Duke Wilhelm the Pious under the direction of a Dutch architect. The great barrel vault of the interior is entirely Renaissance in spirit, its Italian beauty mingling with the heavier seriousness of the Germans.

Not only did Protestant churches cling to the Gothic movement, the façades of many other buildings of the German Renaissance period reflected traditional architectural ideas as well. The stepped gables typical of the north German *Backsteingotik*,

Left Part of the façade of the Cranach House (1549) in Weimar, Thuringia. The decoration above the portal includes the family coat of arms – a winged snake. The artist Lucas Cranach, senior, had his study on the third floor.

Opposite The façade of the town hall (1532) at Saalfeld in Thuringia is built in a traditional style. The staircase tower (left) has some late Gothic elements, especially the pointed arch over the door, while to the right of it is a typical two-storey Renaissance oriel window.

Right Renaissance overdoor at Schloss Heidecksburg, Rudolstadt, Thuringia, with unusually lifelike figures representing Faith, Charity, Hope, Courage and Justice.

Below A typical Weser Renaissance feature is the treatment of oriel windows, which often look like reduced examples of the main façade, as here on the Dempter House (1607) at Hameln, Lower Saxony.

Right The Haus zum Palmbaum at Arnstadt, Thuringia, is named after the tree sprouting from the top of its portal. The Renaissance design, dating from about 1590, had Baroque elements added in 1740 in the form of the broken pediment, on which perch allegorical figures.

Left The main doors of the town hall (1605) at Münden, Lower Saxony. The strong polychromatic ornamentation, and the almost grotesque animal heads, are typical of the Weser Renaissance style.

Left centre The lion fountain (probably about 1600) in the fish market at Offenburg, Baden-Württemberg. The base, with its much cruder carving, is nineteenth century.

Above A stove (1680) in the conference room of the town hall in Regensburg, Bavaria. The figures supporting the base are in the slightly cruder idiom often found in German Renaissance work, while those above are more sophisticated, with the drapery especially giving an early Baroque feel.

or 'Brick Gothic', style, to be seen on the town halls of Lüneburg and Münster, are retained in the stepped gables of Renaissance houses. The gables of the town hall in Brunswick and the façade of St Michael in Munich, both dating from the late sixteenth century, leap upward in vertically accentuated stages, tapering towards the top. The Gothic movement is evident in the vertical emphasis, the Renaissance in the stress on the horizontal mouldings above and under the rows of windows, while the influence of antiquity is evident in the pyramids, obelisques, volutes and niches containing sculptures.

The combination of two styles in German buildings is understandable: the late Gothic movement continued alongside Renaissance development until well into the sixteenth century in Germany, and in the first years of the seventeenth century early examples of Baroque architecture were already to be seen. For this reason it is said that German Renaissance buildings are often either disguised Gothic or tending towards the Baroque. Sometimes German architects simply misunderstood Italian ideas, or they used them only superficially. Often Renaissance decoration is only added to the façade of a building, and the brilliant clarity, the Italian feeling for rhythm and harmony, balance and restraint are lost. Instead the façades of this period seem confused and overladen, with an excessive variety of gables and towers, steps and stairs, galleries, portals and oriels, while the structure itself does not employ the architectural ideas of the Renaissance.

Despite this, however, it will be evident from the pictures in this book that the German Renaissance does have its unmistakable attractions. How original and lively, for instance, is the town hall in Gotha, its square, solid tower with an Italianate dome reflecting the great change that had taken place since the stone lacework of the Gothic towers. The portal on the building is also a fine example of the demonstrative character of the German Renaissance, with its vigorous articulation and imaginative effects. Here you can see clearly how the Christian art of the Middle Ages was superseded by antique mythology: the animals that symbolized medieval supernatural forces are now only allegories on the façade.

It is clear that, for the first time since Europe became the Christian Western world, the source of commissions for buildings had changed. No longer were the bishops the great builders; this role had been taken over by the princes and the munici-

The town hall at Gotha, Thuringia, was built in 1567–77. The south aspect (left) is dominated by a tower with cupola and lantern, while the north is embellished by a magnificent portal (right), flanked by rather incongruous stone reliefs of a lamb (above right) and a crocodile devouring a human head (above far right).

palities. Palaces, town halls, guild halls and middle-class houses were being built. As their political power grew, the princes took over the cultural lead, leaving their castles or changing them into palaces. They laid out their buildings so that the main façades looked inwards onto closed rectangular courtyards. Outwardly the palaces retained their defensive, castle-like character, while the courtyards inside might be surrounded by tiered arcades, with their arches resting on pillars. Inside, the rooms were furnished with ostentatious pride, a demonstration of the dignity of the prince and the skill of the craftsmen. The new feeling for large spaces and perspective created suites of rooms in which several rooms were linked by doors on a central axis. The old palace in Stuttgart, damaged during the Second World War and now restored, was laid out in this way, as was the palace of Neuburg an der Donau and the most important Renaissance building in northern Germany, the palace in Güstrow, which has miraculously survived through all the centuries.

Up to the Gothic period European and German art was Christian, sacred and commissioned by the church. During the Renaissance period secular art took the lead with the construction of palaces, town halls and middle-class houses. The new Protestant churches were hostile to the visual arts, but from the ruins of the Thirty Years' War, from all the blood and tears, religious art re-emerged in triumph, creating Baroque and Rococo churches whose festive piety and religious exuberance are unparalleled.

Above The courtyard of the late-sixteenth-century Schloss Güstrow, Mecklenburg-Western Pomerania, one of the most important Renaissance buildings in north Germany. Italian and Dutch craftsmen worked here, as well as local builders.

Left The Italian influence is evident in the high quality detailing of the arcades and brickwork at Güstrow, seen here at first floor level.

Right In the *Festsaal* (banqueting hall) at Güstrow the reliefs of deer in the window bays carry real horns on their heads.

Left The entrance front of Schloss Bevern (1667), near Holzminden, Lower Saxony.

Far left The courtyard of Schloss Bevern. The rich colours and ornamentation, and the variety of half-timbered work, are typical of the Weser Renaissance style. The staircase tower in the corner has slanting windows which follow the rise of the steps.

Below The Castle Theatre (1685–95) at Celle, Lower Saxony, is the oldest surviving theatre in Germany, and shows how late the Renaissance style persisted in parts of the north. The theatre is still in use today, with its own professional company.

Left Detail of the colonnade apse in the courtyard of the *Stadtresidenz*, or town palace (1540), in Landshut, Bavaria. Among the decorations are Greek deities enclosed in lozenge-shaped mouldings.

BAROQUE AND ROCOCO

The Thirty Years' War had a devastating effect on artistic activity in Germany. It also reduced the population from twenty to thirteen million, and when it was over the Holy Roman Empire existed in name only. When peace was concluded in 1648 there were two hundred principalities, each with its own residence, army and coinage. In addition there were sixty-three ecclesiastical territories, ruled by Roman Catholic archbishops, bishops and abbots, and fifty-five free cities, answerable only to the Emperor. The unity of the Catholic church had also collapsed; instead there were different schisms, which further underlined the fragmentation of the country.

This disarray meant that Germany was slow to absorb the newly emerging art styles, which had begun to flourish in Italy at the end of the sixteenth century. After the terrible loss of power and influence suffered during the Reformation, the Catholic Church was now gathering its spiritual, moral and creative forces for a new attack on the rebellious Protestant states. Its goal was to win these back and strengthen those that had remained loyal to the Catholic faith. New churches were being built and old ones refurbished. They were designed to proclaim the glory of Christianity and the Catholic Church more radiantly than ever before, to affirm the true faith and to display its symbols. The styles created by the Church for this were Baroque and its later form, Rococo. Art history dates these movements roughly between 1600 and 1775. However, Baroque evolved without a clear dividing line from Renaissance and Mannerism, so its beginnings cannot be definitely dated. The final phase is also blurred. In the second half of the eighteenth century we find late Baroque beside Rococo and the emerging early forms of Neoclassicism.

Baroque combined all the arts in a way that was mutually reinforcing. Many frescoes appear lifelike because their themes are continued in an adjacent relief, or interiors are interlinked so as to create constantly changing angles of vision. The dividing line between walls and ceilings is concealed by stucco and wall paintings. Ultimately, the outlines of a room dissolve. *Trompe l'oeil* paintings seem to extend the ceiling almost indefinitely, and mirrors can further confuse the boundaries of a room. Man moves in a new dimension that is both real and unreal. Hence

Above The gigantic high altar (1680) in the parish church at Landsberg am Lech, Bavaria, has gilt decoration of an almost oppressive richness.

Top Ceiling paintings at St Quirin, Tegernsee, representing the Sermon on the Mount.

Above The nave of St Quirin (1684–9) in Tegernsee, Bavaria, is in the more weighty Italian Baroque style, with massive fluted columns and substantial stuccowork especially on the ceiling.

Left Detail of a capital in the nave of St Quirin.

the use of so many *memento mori* and *vanitas* images – a half fearful, half coquettish play with the symbols of transience and death.

The Baroque and Rococo styles encompassed a wide range of art with thousands of variants, lasting for nearly two centuries in many countries. St Peter's in Rome, the Escorial in Spain, the Versailles of the Sun King, Prince Eugen's Belvedere in Vienna, the many Jesuit and Benedictine monastery and pilgrimage churches that were built from Europe to South

America all testify to the unmistakable, uninhibited wealth of the Baroque style. The force of the Renaissance was not all spent, in that its formal language, the vocabulary of its architecture, was adopted, intensified and taken to extremes of energy and strength to create a new language and style. Classical severity and balance gave way to freedom and static art to rhythm, while the calm stability of rooms dissolved in flowing and swinging movement. Nineteenth-century critics scornfully referred to

forms as 'baroque' and distorted, because they objected to the sensuous extravagant gestures and the preference for voluptuous forms.

Indeed, everything in the Baroque was designed for the grand effect. The façade grew steadily in importance, with the addition of relief decoration, figure work, columns and pilasters. The surfaces of façades moved rhythmically in convex and concave curves, like a membrane that is pushed out or sucked in by the space behind. The Renaissance had declared a rational human scale to be the ideal basis for its system of measurement and proportion; the Baroque took this to perfection, and then to absurdity. Numbers and dimensions were no longer measurable; architectural relationships became much more complicated and the calculations more complex. But no effort was to be visible in the Baroque, one thing was to emerge from the next, easily and seemingly by chance. Hence, for example, an oval vestibule finds a response in a convex façade, which seems to be moving outward like a living organism to evade the pressure from within.

The beginnings of this movement were already to be found in neighbouring countries when, a generation after the Thirty Years' War, German Baroque began to flourish. Church architecture borrowed Italian ideas, creating in Catholic parts of the country the style of Austrian and south German Baroque. With its churches, monasteries and ecclesiastical residences Baroque dominated the landscape south of the Main, and it was soon apparent that, although Germany's creative forces might have been suppressed by the long war, they had certainly not been paralysed or destroyed.

Baroque architects concentrated on eliminating the appearance of heaviness from a building and creating a sense of swinging or floating perfection. Pillars stand out, doubled and tripled, as if they were muscles holding up the vault above them. Columns and volutes, arches and mouldings add to the upward movement. The altar is not only the spiritual centre of the church, it is also its principal focus, so all architectural movement comes together here and continues upwards. One of these great altars is to be seen in the church of Mary's Ascension (*Mariä Himmelfahrt*) in Landsberg am Lech. With its dancing, gold-robed angels, twisted columns, curved architraves and dramatically majestic size, it seems to be bearing the nave of the church aloft and almost bursting through the vault of the ceiling.

Left Italians were responsible for the stuccowork and remodelled interior (1676–98) of the originally Gothic town church in Celle, Lower Saxony.

Below Detail of the decoration in the south aisle of the Church of the Birth of the Virgin at Rottenbuch with (left) two putti suspended above the side-altar.

Right The nave of the former Augustinian Church of the Birth of the Virgin at Rottenbuch, near Schongau in Bavaria. The stuccowork, executed around 1745, marks a transition from Baroque to early Rococo. The frescoes depict scenes from the life of St Augustine. In the foreground are two putti mounted on the edge of the organ loft.

Opposite The nave at Rottenbuch seen from the north aisle, with part of the pulpit in the foreground.

Left Detail of the interior of the Wies pilgrimage church in Bavaria (built by D. Zimmermann 1746–54). The cool white columns, in the nave near the organ loft, have comparatively restrained ornamentation.

Right The rich Rococo decoration of the Wies church achieves its maximum concentration of shape and colour in this area above the high altar. Attention is particularly focused on B. A. Albrecht's painting of the Incarnation of Christ.

Left Detail of the Rococo pulpit (about 1750) in the monastery church at Steingaden, Bavaria. Animal figures alternate with cherubic heads against a background of elaborate scrollwork.

Right Ceiling painting above the organ loft at Steingaden. Unusually, the subject matter is secular, showing parts of the church and monastery under construction.

Pages 86–7 Falkenlust, the small hunting lodge built by Francois Cuvilliés in 1729–40 in the grounds of Schloss Augustusburg at Brühl, near Cologne. Strangely, it is enclosed by a small ring fence, as if it were a town house.

The pilgrimage church Die Wies near Steingaden in the hilly Alpine foreland of Bavaria was consecrated in 1754 and is pure Rococo. Like many German Rococo churches, it does not follow an international style of architecture, it is an independent German creation. The church grew out of local community life; farmers of the area between the Ammer and Lech rivers had asked for a church to be built as a monument to a miracle they had experienced. The church was built by local architects and stuccowork artists, and the people loved it. Two generations later they saved it when it was to be pulled down during the 'secularization' (dissolution of churches) of 1803. Outwardly simple, the church interior presents an overwhelmingly powerful impression, and in its interplay of light, colour and spatial movement it is one of the finest works of art on German soil. The broad oval of the nave passes without a break into a long choir. Above this, supported by eight double columns, rises a magnificent painted vault. It is as if the architecture only consisted of stucco and colour. The church walls are so white that they reflect light and mirror it back again, lending even greater luminosity to the foaming white and gold of the rocaille stucco and delicate frescoes. Curving groups of windows and smaller openings allow the light to flood into the oval space, and as the sun traverses the sky its movement is drawn into the body of the church. The arches under the vault swing in dancing curves from one pair of columns to the next. Any intensification of this architectural hymn of praise, designed to give a taste of heaven on earth, would be hard to imagine.

The first-floor landing of the staircase hall of the Benedictine abbey at Gengenbach, Baden-Württemberg, in the Black Forest. Dating from 1750, it has recently been restored to its original condition and colours. The splendour of the plasterwork and paintings was created less for the benefit of the resident monks than as a stage for the courtly ceremony attendant on visits by more exalted church dignitaries.

Right In a typically fantastical detail of the Rococo plasterwork at Gengenbach abbey, a bird-like dragon confronts a snake's head emerging from the wall.

Below A *trompe l'oeil* doorway in the staircase hall at Gengenbach.

Right This detail from the Great Banqueting Hall at the Baroque Schloss Leitheim, near Donauwörth, Bavaria, shows church and state in opposition. The grotesque heads represent the sacred (left, smiling) and the profane.

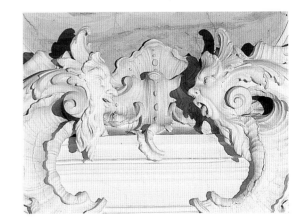

Above Schloss Leitheim is linked by a covered arcade to this church, which is of similar size to the residence. This reflected these buildings' original purpose as both a place of worship and a summer residence for the Cistercian abbey at Kaisheim.

Right The façade of the church of St Johannes (built by D. Zimmermann in 1741) in Landsberg am Lech, Bavaria. The comparatively restrained articulation hides an ornate Rococo interior.

Far right Mariental monastery (about 1740), north of Zittau in south-east Saxony, and on the border with Czechoslovakia, is in the Bohemian Baroque style. With its rich colours and almost oriental splendour, it dominates the valley like some Indian rajah's palace.

The Rococo monastery libraries of central and southern Germany sometimes create a more powerful impression than their associated churches, perhaps because the statues especially are relatively restrained and free from the stylized exaggeration of gesture and expression often found in the churches. Here at Wiblingen monastery (about 1750) near Ulm, the first floor gallery of the library (right and opposite) is supported by red and blue marble columns, sometimes in pairs, with life-sized figures representing intellectual and spiritual knowledge and other virtues. The doors giving access to the gallery (opposite below) are disguised as recessed panels, containing statues similar to those on the floor below.

It became difficult to tell whether residences had been commissioned by secular or ecclesiastical princes. The architectural career of François Cuvilliés started when the Elector Max Emanuel of Bavaria returned from exile in Paris with Cuvilliés as his court dwarf. The elector had had him trained in Paris, thus paving the way for one of the most brilliant architects of the Rococo. Cuvilliés built the Amalienburg and the Residence Theatre in Munich for the Elector of Bavaria with the same beauty and elegance as he built the palace of Augustusburg and the *maison de plaisir*, Falkenlust, in Brühl, for the elector's son the Archbishop Clemens August. Hardly in keeping with his spiritual task but entirely in the style of the time, the archbishop used the intimate, blue and white Rococo palace, which is linked by an avenue with the episcopal residence of Augustusburg in Brühl, as a hunting lodge, for festivities and his mistresses.

More modest and provincial, but typical precisely for that reason is the ecclesiastical residence of Leitheim near Donauwörth. It was the summer residence of the Cistercian order in Kaisheim and it clearly shows the interlinking of secular and spiritual requirements. The residence is linked by a covered arcade to the church. The interiors of both buildings are decorated in the lively splendour of Baroque and Rococo. The sumptuous stucco in the rooms, the themes of the ceiling paintings – *Day Driving out Night*, *The Five Senses* – and the architectural play with light and landscape outside the windows show that the Cistercians' delight in this ensemble was not only of a spiritual nature. The Benedictine monastery in Gengenbach also combines monastic life with the courtly elegance and display of the Rococo period. The stairway is like that of a noble palace. The abbot's coat of arms is held by two putti, Rococo wrought-iron railings dance up the stairs and on the walls frescoes imitate doors and side stairs to make the room look bigger. The monastery had political and economic tasks to perform as well as its spiritual work, and the abbot wanted to present himself to the world in the contemporary style.

Thus religious building activity was not only limited to the construction of churches, and in the eighteenth century, for the first time since the Reformation, new monasteries were built. They were enclosed but extensive, open to enjoyment, intellectually active and architecturally of such powerfully

Overleaf left The entrance of the abbey library at Bad Schussenried, between Ulm and Lake Constance (Bodensee) in Baden-Württemberg.

Overleaf right A corner of the Bad Schussenried library, with a painting of an open book in a flamboyant surround on the ceiling. The bookcases are in the same style as the entrance door.

Page 95 In the Bad Schussenried library, built between 1755 and 1766, the first-floor gallery that winds around the library has a Rococo balustrade, which is supported by pairs of columns adorned alternately by effigies of fathers of the church (as here) and cherubim in burlesque costumes.

bold conception that they resemble great palaces. Weingarten, Banz, Ottobeuren, St Florian and Melk, for example, have magnificent halls, theatres and princely reception rooms for the senior clergy in the monasteries around their churches. Particular architectural care was lavished on the libraries, which are like magnificent temples of wisdom. Libraries especially reflect the changing times. In the Middle Ages monasteries and ecclesiastical foundations were the only depositories of knowledge; then, when many monasteries were dissolved during the Reformation, the libraries also lost their homes. Instead, princes, municipalities and universities began to collect books and build up libraries of their own. When monasteries again began to be built in the eighteenth century and the strictness of monastic life was relaxed somewhat, the spirit of the Baroque age found particular expression in the libraries.

During the eighteenth century there was a surge of interest in knowledge and scientific research as a result of the secularization of thought and life, even within the church, and library rooms like those at St Peter near Freiburg and Wiblingen near Ulm are impressive testimonies to this. Bad Schussenried's famous library combines both learning and art. The sparkling grace of its stuccowork and frescoes almost

At Neuburg an der Donau, Bavaria, the library furnishings and bookshelves (right) – surmounted by elaborately carved coats of arms and putti (below right) – originate from the former Cistercian monastery at Kaisheim. After Kaisheim's dissolution they were transported to Neuburg and rebuilt in what was then a monastery building, beneath a superb Rococo ceiling.

makes us forget that this room was intended for the furtherance of enlightenment and the scientific illumination of the earth. No dark leather books line the shelves, only what seem to be rows of books in the pastel tones of the Rococo but are in fact book spines painted onto the glass panels to complete the decorative ensemble.

A clock hangs down from the ceiling of the staircase hall of the monastery of St Peter near Freiburg. Its elaborate, asymmetrical frame, with porcelain putti clambering around it in delicate pastel tones, is characteristic of the Rococo period. But the clock itself is also a kind of symbol for the whole age, typically combining systems of thought with artistic trends in the most elegant way. The philosopher Gottfried Wilhelm Leibniz had seen the cosmos as a mechanism that functioned according to strict mathematical laws. The body and soul of man,

Left The Rococo monastery library at St Peter, near Freiburg im Breisgau in the Black Forest, was built in 1750 under the direction of the well-known architect Peter Thumb, from Constance on the Swiss border. Around the first floor gallery stand Matthias Faller's allegorical statues representing the arts and sciences.

Below left Of the same style and period is the clock in the staircase hall of the St Peter monastery, adorned with climbing putti and scrollwork.

he explained, were related like two clocks which were so excellently crafted that they always showed exactly the same time. Clocks were highly prestigious on account of their technical innovations and because they could be made with a wide variety of impressive materials. Consequently in Dresden, Berlin and many other centres in Germany a new age of clockmaking began.

At the turn of the seventeenth century secular architecture in Germany had also reached European rank. The political circumstances were favourable, for the Austrian monarchy had emerged strengthened from the Turkish wars. The German princes were also in victorious mood, as they had fought with Austria and shared its triumph. All over the Holy Roman Empire German courts flourished like larger and smaller clocks ticking away in the same spirit and style, and each entirely self-absorbed. Political

Left A corner of the *Festsaal* (banqueting hall) in Schloss Friedenstein (about 1690), Gotha, Thuringia. The massive Baroque statues and columns are overhung by equally substantial ceiling reliefs.

Right and below A corner and a detail of the *Spiegelraum* (mirror room), built about 1780, in Schloss Heidecksburg, Rudolstadt, Thuringia, which also houses a fine porcelain collection.

absolutism had come from France and was now firmly established in Germany, and following the French model the Baroque palace had become the symbol of secular absolutism; this was the art of kings who believed they ruled by the grace of God. Hence secular or profane art claimed equality with religious art, and certainly in Germany a hectic rivalry developed between ecclesiastical and secular rulers trying to outdo each other with the same materials.

Some features of the Baroque and Rococo periods are to be found mainly in palaces and royal residences rather than in churches, such as chinoiserie, for instance, which spread from the seafaring nations to Germany. The Dutch East India Company had made the Netherlands rich, and the British East India Company laid the basis for the economic upturn in Britain. The allure of the Far East was

spread by painted silks, porcelain, wallpapers, lacquer and mother-of-pearl – all the luxury goods that enriched the Baroque interiors of many residences with their exotic attractions. Outside, pagodas, tea houses, bell pavilions and hanging bamboo bridges were built in the gardens. Porcelain was particularly highly prized, and anyone who could afford it created special rooms to display these wares from the Far East, as for instance at the Neues Palais in Arnstadt. The German nobility saw in this a continuance of the humanist concept of the curio cabinets, the custom that had been familiar since Renaissance times for collecting and showing strange things from all over the world to extend and enrich knowledge.

Another feature of the Baroque interior is the skilful use of mirrors, which can have the effect of making a room look larger. Later, in the Rococo period, this principle was taken to such extremes that rooms almost seemed to dissolve in light; reflections and counter-reflections were so cleverly manipulated that the surrounding walls hardly seem to exist at all.

Among the great achievements of secular Baroque architecture were the stairways of palaces. In the Renaissance period the staircase was often not much more than a simple spiral, but in the Baroque period it became an important part of court ceremonies, the place where the courtiers assembled for festivities, and where both the individual and the entire ensemble could be effectively displayed. Ascending to the *bel étage* (first floor) or descending into the gardens, the visitor experienced an ever-changing sequence of turns, views, openings, raised levels and overlapping spaces before emerging into the light – the brilliant lights of the banqueting rooms above or the natural light of the gardens below.

The princes were, as already noted, the great secular builders of the age. Many towns had not yet recovered from the wounds of the Thirty Years' War and the new style had not made much impression on them. However, one particularly fine example of Baroque urban architecture is the Böttingerhaus in Judengasse in Bamberg. The courtyard is energetic Baroque of the Main-Franconian region, and it is an impressive illustration of the local differences to be found in Germany. The voluptuous, acanthus-leaf ornamentation is still entirely in the manner of the seventeenth century, and it recalls the florid style that brought the German Renaissance to a close and marked the transition to the new age. The hermae on the portal and in the courtyard are full-blown

Left The *Festsaal* (banqueting hall) of the Neues Palais at Arnstadt, Thuringia. The ceiling, executed between 1732 and 1737 by Tobias Müller of Rudolstadt, is in the late Baroque style, as are the corner apse and pilasters.

Opposite The Porcelain Room (1735) in the Neues Palais, one of the finest surviving examples of its kind, houses an important collection of seventeenth- and eighteenth-century porcelain from the Far East.

The Böttinger House in Judengasse, Bamberg, Bavaria, was built in 1707–13. The arcaded courtyard (right) has delicate stucco patterns on its ceiling, while the powerful figures of the statues (below) surrounding the entrance above the courtyard are hardly contained by their somewhat cramped urban surroundings.

Right Rococo façade of a town house on Untere Brücke street, Bamberg.

Below The main street-entrance to the Böttinger House.

eighteenth-century Baroque figures, powerful and full of tense energy.

An important contribution to the German Baroque and Rococo styles in the east of the country came at this time from Prussia, which was just emerging as a major power. During the seventeenth and eighteenth centuries Prussia arose from among the German states and began to compete with the old-established imperial Austria. Since 1701 the Elector of Brandenburg had been able to call himself 'King in Prussia'. Frederick I, as he then became, the first Hohenzollern king, was a ruler entirely in the spirit of the Baroque, and with the assistance of the sculptor and architect Andreas Schlüter he transformed the face of the new state, giving it dignity and presence, and laying out Berlin as a Baroque city.

The imperial Baroque of Austria and the royal Baroque of Prussia have often been compared. Vienna is said to be all joyous harmony, while Berlin, for all its Baroque exuberance, has a certain disharmony or harshness. The palace of Charlottenburg, begun by Frederick I in 1695 for his consort Sophie Charlotte and continued by Frederick II, certainly does not deserve such epithets. Its restrained elegance is not off-putting but on the contrary dignified and welcoming. Sophie Charlotte had expressed a desire for a palace out in the countryside during a hunting party, and it was here that the most interesting people of the time collected around a queen who herself was highly educated, intelligent and a skilful writer. When she died the palace was given her name, but the intellectual life in its rooms died with her. Her son, Frederick William I, who certainly justified his nickname 'Soldier King', ordered it to be closed. He hated luxury, festivities and 'philosophical fiddle-faddle', and had the flowers in the Baroque gardens replaced by rows of cabbages.

Despite his animosity to such activities the Soldier King indirectly and unintentionally made a great contribution to German culture. He left his son Frederick II, later called Frederick the Great, an intact, well-organized and economically sound, authoritarian state in 1740 and so created the basis on which his successor was able to build up one of the most superior, intellectual and cultivated courts of his time in Potsdam. 'Friderician Rococo' was created in Potsdam with a little palace of supreme artistry called 'Sanssouci' (1745–7). The construction of an intimate *petite maison* was in keeping with the spirit of the time. It was as if rulers were wearying

of the great gestures, the public show and grandiose ceremonies that had characterized the Baroque in every aspect of art and life. The Rococo brought a desire to withdraw into a luxurious retreat, which would appropriately be called 'Eremitage', 'Monrepos', 'Solitude' or, as here, 'Sanssouci'.

A single-storey, broadly based building in pavilion style, with a projecting centre part that is semicircular in shape and crowned with a cupola, Sanssouci opens into the gardens through great windows that reach down to the ground. The gardens lead down in six terraces of glass-covered orchards and vineyards to the level ground below. The interiors are French in inspiration, and for all their luxury they are not

magnificent and imposing but exquisite, light and serene. The carved, gilt decoration covers the walls with a sure feeling for free rhythmic effect. Equally impressive and opulent are the interiors of the adjacent Neue Kammern, originally built as an orangery in restrained, mid-century Baroque but later redecorated in flamboyant Rococo style.

In Sanssouci the ideas of the Rococo were beginning to mix with those of the Enlightenment. In the best traditions of absolutism Frederick was still able to look out over the world and see the lands he ruled lying at his feet, but unlike his forebears he did not feel that he was placed on the throne by the grace of God; he saw it as due to the chance of his birth.

Consequently the task of ruling was a constant challenge to him: he had to be at once supreme promoter, controller, administrator, diplomat and army commander; in short, he was constrained always to be the best at everything. This effort induced an almost apocalyptic mood in him, and this is nowhere so clearly expressed as in his choice of the name 'Sanssouci', the place where one day he would be free from care, when all the work of ruling was done. Hence he ordered that he should be buried at Sanssouci, on the top step of his terraces, where the first ray of the morning sun would touch the soil of his garden. This last command remained unfulfilled until after Germany's reunification.

The magnificent suite of rooms known as the *Neue Kammern* (new apartments), in the garden of Schloss Sanssouci at Potsdam, was created in 1771–4 in late Rococo style as overflow accommodation for guests at the court. Shown here is the Ovid Gallery.

Above left The south aspect of Schloss Charlottenburg (around 1700), Berlin, which started off as a commission to build a small country house. The projecting central area, with its differently articulated windows, was added later to provide support for the massive dome.

Above One of the reliefs in the Ovid Gallery, depicting the legend of Danae and Jupiter.

Left The exterior of the Neue Kammern. The building was originally constructed as an orangery.

NEOCLASSICISM

Frederick the Great's last building had astonished the world. After the Seven Years' War Prussia was thought to be impoverished and exhausted; instead, immediately the war was over, in 1763, Frederick the Great began to build his Neues Palais, and by 1769 it was finished. It was a huge and imposing palace, harking back to the late Baroque in style, and the king spared no expense on it. He may later have talked about it light-heartedly but he was annoyed that it was not his palace that was on everyone's lips in Berlin society. Instead, people were talking about a country seat that had just been built in the provinces by a 'petty prince', 'in the new manner', as the king noted with rancour.

The 'petty prince' was Leopold III, Frederick Franz of Anhalt-Dessau, and the 'new manner' was Neoclassicism. It challenged the frivolity and excess, the shells and asymmetrical fancies of the Rococo with its clear, simple lines, with cube and cylinder, circle and square. Prince Franz's palace, Wörlitz near Dessau (completed 1776), is held to be the building that established Neoclassicism in Germany. His architect, Freiherr von Erdmannsdorff, took an innovative step by abandoning the curving façade, the rich relief ornamentation and the *cour d'honneur* of the traditional Baroque palace and replacing them with a clearly structured, simple villa. Relief decoration is extremely sparse. The individual parts of the building are clearly demarcated; the smooth flat surface of the walls is emphasized and the decoration is restrained. The façade is dominated by a great,

nobly proportioned, columned portico across the entrance. The roof has an unusual addition: a belvedere in the form of an additional storey reached by an inside spiral staircase. At the top the visitor finds himself leaning on a railing like that on a ship, looking out over the misty woods and fields stretching away at his feet. The nautical reference is a strange architectural conceit for a house in a small German state that was nowhere near the sea.

The belvedere in fact evoked the journey Prince Franz had undertaken with his architect Erdmannsdorff to Great Britain. Britain was then regarded as the most advanced country in Europe – politically, economically and culturally – and the prince and his architect wanted to collect ideas for a complete work of art in the spirit of the Enlightenment, which they hoped to construct in the plains around the Elbe in

Left Schloss Wörlitz, near Dessau, was modelled on the eighteenth-century English country house at Claremont in Surrey and was Germany's first Neoclassical building.

Right The dining room at Wörlitz has similar Corinthian columns to those supporting the entrance portico. Here they frame a statue of Bacchus, which is a copy of an antique original in Rome.

Dessau-Wörlitz. The prince's desire for reform was fired by the conviction that the world could be changed if the rules of reason and simple taste were followed. Buildings should no longer demonstrate power and glory or be filled with exquisite works of art to indulge the owner; buildings should educate, teach and inspire. Beauty should certainly be combined with the useful and practical, and the land should be developed so that the people could profit as well. On the water meadows of the Elbe Prince Franz created a textbook of the Enlightenment, a centre of education and a model agricultural project; he used the most modern methods and set architectural patterns for the future.

Wörlitz is an example of how ideas can be expressed in architecture. A 'pantheon', a seat for all the gods, was erected as a demonstration of religious tolerance. Tolerance was really practised in Anhalt-Dessau, and Prince Franz also had a synagogue built, so close to the church that both buildings could be seen at a glance. Another important postulate of the Enlightenment was to honour nature and beautify it where possible. In the park at Wörlitz the first warning sign in Germany, a column decorated with reliefs, asks visitors to protect nature. 'Walkers are requested to have thought for nature and art and not to harm their works,' says the inscription. Two ideas that were formative in the new style are interlinked here – Neoclassicism saw it as the aim of art not only to imitate antiquity but also to imitate nature. This followed the 'back to nature' doctrines of Jean Jacques Rousseau, and for this reason the French philosopher was enthusiastically honoured at Wörlitz: his grave on an island of poplars in the park at Ermenonville in France was recreated by placing a memorial stone and an urn, surrounded by a circle of poplar trees, in the middle of an island on the lake at Wörlitz.

The gardens at Wörlitz also contain what is called the Gothic House, although it has little in common with any medieval style of building. It is a product of the Romantic movement, and it takes up Romantic perceptions and combines these with the nature around it. The prince loved the 'picturesque style' he had seen in England. The twilight mood of some of the rooms in the house does recall the spirit of the Middle Ages, with its monasteries and knights, as this was then understood. The panes of glass in the windows of the Geistliches Kabinett do in fact date from the fifteenth century; the writer Lavater had bought them in Switzerland. But the house also contains elements of personal, national significance, for the prince put on display the Anhalt collection of paintings built up by his ancestors, and among the major pieces were works by Cranach and his school, which established a link with the German Reformation.

The Classical tradition of two thousand years of culture was seen as part of the present, it was a living culture, and not only in Wörlitz. Winckelmann had published his *Gedanken über die Nachahmung der griechischen Werke in der Malerei und der Bild-hauerkunst* (Thoughts on the Imitation of Greek Works in Painting and Sculpture) in 1755 and his *Geschichte der Kunst des Altertums* (History of the Art of Antiquity) in 1764, in which he demanded an unconditional return to the values of antiquity. Under the influence of antiquity art was seen more with the eyes of the sculptor. Only the pure Doric line, the noble contour, the male body refined in marble were acceptable. Interiors and parks were decorated everywhere with reproductions and casts

of antique statues. Favourites were Ganymede and Apollo with powerful and elegant figures in noble and relaxed postures.

Another event helped to create a veritable mania for all things antique. Since 1748 the Roman provincial towns of Pompeii and Herculaneum, which had been buried by masses of lava and ash from a volcanic eruption in the year AD 79, had been systematically excavated, and the astonished and admiring world began to learn about everyday life in antiquity. Travellers to Italy were returning with new ideas and decorating their houses in the Graeco-Roman style. To name only some of the countless examples, there are the Marble Palace in Potsdam, the Neoclassical wing of Schloss Friedenstein in Gotha and, as late as the mid-nineteenth century, the Villa Lindenhof on Lake Constance.

The revolutionary turmoil and wars at the turn of the eighteenth century should not conceal the fact that other revolutions were taking place beside the political upheavals. Electricity and gas were beginning to conquer Europe and light the big cities.

Machines, mostly from England at first, were heralding the industrial age. New needs were awakened, new luxuries and new poverty created. As the century went on, the middle class became more influential and prosperous, and a new class emerged, the unionized workers.

Where was art in all this? Talleyrand once mentioned sadly that in 1789 the sweetness went from life forever. That was certainly true of the Baroque and its elegant finale, Rococo. The church and the nobility, the great builders and purchasers of that period, had lost much of their possessions. But building went on. Indeed, an enormous demand for building developed in the main cities and seats of government – parliament buildings, offices, theatres, museums, academies, stock exchanges, memorials and mausoleums were all required. Most of these public buildings were designed in the Palladian manner, in the Neoclassical spirit, as had happened much earlier in England. William Hogarth had ironically commented as early as 1753 in his *Analysis of Beauty* that, if a modern architect were to build a palace in Lapland or the West Indies, Palladio would be his model – no architect would dare to take a single step without the Quattro Libri.

The strict adherence to the architectural ideas of ancient Greece and Rome ushered in a new age.

Left Detail of the painted walls in the Pompeian Room (about 1805) in the Neoclassical west wing of Schloss Friedenstein, Gotha, Thuringia, showing the application of antique stylistic forms.

Right A view from the Blue Room (foreground) at Friedenstein, with an anatomical sculpture, into the Marble Room with a statue representing Diana. Both sculptures are by Jean Antoine Houdon.

Far left The *Geistliches Kabinett* (spiritual room) in the Gothic House in the park of Schloss Wörlitz. Late eighteenth-century Neo-Gothic arches frame earlier stained glass windows, mostly made in Switzerland, and a collection of even older altar paintings, dating from around 1500.

Buildings of clearly articulated monumentality were created, following mathematical rules of measurement and also exercising restraint in their use of colour and ornamentation. Their façades were defined by the portal or the Greek temple front with its triangular pediment. Flat pilasters and bands divided the body of the building, and the more prominent elements were accentuated by a stronger application of columns, pillars or mouldings. In their reserve and severity the buildings sometimes seem cool or even artificial.

Germany only fully turned to the new style of architecture towards the end of the eighteenth century, but then the progress was rapid and thorough. In Prussia the new movement met the need of the state for a suitable capital city to reflect its new position in the world. Frederick II had tried to set up a new 'Protestant metropolis' against the old-established, Catholic Vienna and find an individual style for its expression. But Friderician Baroque, the first representative style in Prussia, had remained eclectic, apart from the highly individual interior

decoration of the palaces. Neoclassicism came at a timely moment to fill the gap and give Prussia a style unencumbered by the historical past, with which the rapidly growing state could identify. The Palladian style, in particular, with its structural sobriety, clear forms, economy and discipline perfectly suited the Prussian state, and it was a happy coincidence that the style of the time so ideally matched the Prussian catalogue of virtues. Thus Prussia built in the style that all Europe had adopted, only rather more so than other states. Classical architecture with pediment, pilasters and columns also met the taste of a society that had to come to terms with the restoration of conservative forces in Europe after the Congress of Vienna in 1815.

Only Greek architecture could give exemplary expression to the relationship between support and load, said Karl Friedrich Schinkel, appointed to the office of Director of Building in Prussia in 1815. It was fortunate and fruitful that Prussia's crown prince, who was to become Frederick William IV, was an intellectual, art-loving man, himself a gifted

Villa Lindenhof (1842–5), situated in a small park leading down to the north shore of Lake Constance, near Lindau, combines Greek and Roman stylistic elements. The Corinthian columns supporting the bay window (opposite above) are surmounted by more severe, square ones on the balcony above, while an ornate frieze runs along the top of the façade, under the roof overhang. In the former billiards room (left) a stylized figure with veils and cymbals dances against a background of Pompeian red, under a delicately painted *trompe l'oeil* canopy. The wall paintings in other rooms (opposite below) are likewise based on Greek and Roman models, and include horse-drawn chariots and dancing couples in their subject matter.

architect. Partly through his support Schinkel was able to imprint on Berlin the stamp of his far-reaching plans, which combined classical proportions with Neo-Gothic imagination. Although many of his projects were never realized, Schinkel shaped Berlin like no other architect, and Neoclassical Berlin, with the Lustgarten, the Altes Museum, the Schlossbrücke, the Neue Wache, the Werdersche Markt and its church, the Bauakademie, Gendarmenmarkt and Schauspielhaus, was his work, as were many of the parks, squares and streets.

Schinkel's finest and most significant work is the Museum für Alte Kunst (1822–30) in Berlin, usually referred to as the 'Altes Museum'. The ground plan is strikingly simple and clear. The dominant space is the rotunda in the centre, which like so many of its kind was modelled on the Pantheon in Rome and was designed to house the most valuable items in the antiquities collection. It is surrounded by display rooms which run round all four sides of the museum building and enclose the two interior courtyards beside the rotunda. The Altes Museum also has an interesting staircase layout. After passing through the long columned portico that forms the façade, and on through the narrow hall and four more mighty pillars, the visitor can choose between two routes, either going on into the centre, the rotunda, or ascending a staircase from the open hall. The stairs are at first narrow and dark, but each step was designed to offer new and different insights, with views at the top into the rotunda, to the picture-covered walls of the hall or through the columns into the open air and the Lustgarten beneath.

After the Second World War Schinkel's architecture was rejected for a long time because Hitler's architect, Albert Speer, had been able to misuse it for gigantic building projects devoid of intellectual content. Speer had used Neoclassical forms to present Hitler's fascist displays, but the internal stairway in the Altes Museum is a fine example of the difference between the two architects and the psychological effect they achieved. In the Altes Museum the visitor ascends from the shadows to the light; at every step he sees and experiences new things; he lives and learns at every stage. Typical fascist buildings, on the other hand, for all their Neoclassical borrowings, are like fortresses. They have impenetrable façades and demand subjection. They are demonstrations of power, and were intended to terrify and oppress.

Part of the pantheon rotunda which forms the heart of the Altes Museum, Berlin. The gallery is supported by a peristyle of Greek Corinthian columns.

Left The *Vorhalle* (entrance portico) of Schinkel's Altes Museum (1823–30) in Berlin. The walls were formerly decorated with paintings of scenes from Greek mythology, which were destroyed in the Second World War. It was not practicable to re-create these during the post-war restoration of the museum, so the surfaces were repainted in the strong orange-red which was one of the colours favoured by Schinkel.

A general view of the Altes Museum rotunda, showing the coffered ceiling and the floor, which was designed to look like an Italian marble pavement.

Above Two putti, growing in relief out of the surrounding foliage, adorn this small roundel (about 1850) above the entrance door to the Neue Kammern at Sanssouci, Potsdam.

Right The orangery (1851–7) in the gardens of Sanssouci was designed by two of Schinkel's protégés, following Italian Renaissance models.

Jagdschloss Granitz (below), on the island of Rügen off the north-east Baltic coast, was commissioned in 1836 by the newly created Prince von Putbus to show off his elevated status. The dominating central tower, 38 metres (125 ft) high, was designed by Schinkel, and contains a striking wrought-iron spiral staircase (left).

Neoclassicism on a more intimate scale in the grounds of Schloss Kleinglienicke, between Berlin and Potsdam: parts of a Venetian Carthusian monastery (above and left) which were brought there and reconstructed as the *Klosterhöfchen*, and Schinkel's Rotunda (above right).

It is a strange coincidence that at the other end of the German Reich, in Bavaria, a similarly fruitful partnership between a ruler and his architect was evolving. King Ludwig I of Bavaria was a frustrated architect, like the crown prince of Prussia, and he was also a fanatical lover of art. It was said that he did not care if his children ate rye bread if he could spend millions on museums, temples and palaces. It was his ambition to change the cosy residence town of Munich, which had less than 50,000 inhabitants, into a royal European capital, and in doing so recreate the most sublime parts of Athens, Paestum, or ancient Rome. It was better to assemble an imitation of all that was finest in antiquity, he believed, than to create an original that was less sublime.

His architect was Leo von Klenze, who was also a painter and an archaeologist. Klenze worked at a time when, as the century went on, Neoclassicism was becoming more imbued with nationalistic fervour. After the experiences of the twentieth century and the tragedy brought on the world and on Germany itself by nationalism and popular fanaticism, it is hard to do justice to the works of Klenze that are dedicated to nationalistic and heroic moods and feelings. Bombast and nationalism were certainly not only a German phenomenon, but many a German will nevertheless wish, as he looks today at Valhalla and Kelheim, Klenze's great national monuments, that they incorporated rather less of the heroic stance and rather more distance.

While still a crown prince facing Napoleon's armies in Germany, Ludwig I had taken the decision to set up a German pantheon. Between 1830 and 1841 a Doric temple was created for 'Germans of great fame and renown', and set on wooded banks above Donaustauf, in a beautiful landscape. It was given the name Valhalla, the hall of the dead in old Nordic sagas, where the god of death, Odin, summons the souls of fallen warriors for their last, great honour. In the polychrome marble interior of Ludwig's Valhalla the heroic souls are represented by busts, and some are of outstanding quality. Which Germans were great enough to be summoned to Valhalla was decided by the king himself, and we see that royalty and the nobility had more claim to renown than ordinary people, south Germans more than north Germans, Catholics more than Protestants, and Martin Luther, who did indeed do little for Bavaria, is not here at all. There were some in Germany who demanded that a German national monument should be built in the German style, that is, Neo-Gothic. But Ludwig I

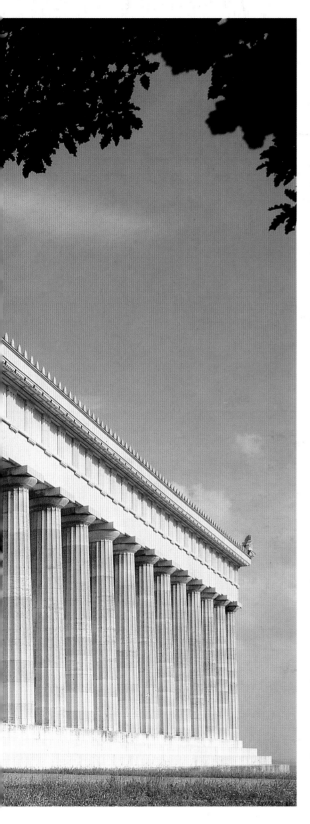

Left Valhalla, on a commanding site overlooking the Danube near Regensburg, Bavaria, was built by Leo von Klenze in 1830–41. Based on Greek models, it has fifty-two Doric columns and was dedicated to famous Germans.

Right and below The Liberation Hall at Kelheim near Regensburg was begun in the Byzantine style by F. Gärtner but was eventually completed in the 'Antique Roman' style by Leo von Klenze in 1863. The exterior (right) recalls the Tomb of Theodorich in Ravenna, while the interior (below) is reminiscent of the Pantheon in Rome.

would accept nothing but the Graeco-Roman style. Anything else was only 'building' and not 'architecture', said Klenze.

Standing on the ancient ruins of Tiryns in Greece, the king decided in 1836 to give the Germans another national monument. It was to commemorate the Battle of the Nations near Leipzig in 1813 and the Wars of Liberation (1813–15) against Napoleon. The project took nearly thirty years to complete. During this time the king had an affair with the beautiful and fiery Lola Montez, and had to abdicate. He went on building privately, and in 1863 the work was finished. It is a huge, cylindrical structure on the Michaelsberg near Kelheim, bare, proud and windowless, more like an outsize grave-mound. It is surrounded by eighteen heavy supports on which are stone-carved female forms in antique dress and hairstyles. Inside, the walls are polychrome marble as in Valhalla, and the only light enters through the cupola. Thirty-four winged goddesses of victory in Carrera marble, representing the German states, stand in different poses in a circle, holding hands. Shortly before his death the architect took the king, now abdicated and himself an old man, into the completed Liberation Hall. The king burst into tears, not because it was so German, but because it was more beautiful than he had ever dared hope.

THE MODERN MOVEMENT

As the nineteenth century progressed, the face of the civilized world changed more than it had ever changed before. The industrial revolution affected not only economic conditions but every aspect of life. Within a few decades many cities grew to be great metropolises, with industrial areas, working-class quarters and residential districts extending their boundaries on a hitherto unknown scale. Consequently the architects of the time found themselves facing new and unusual tasks. They tackled them initially in the conventional manner; their buildings are technically masterful but stylistically orientated towards the past. The restrained calm of Neoclassicism was over, and as the century drew to a close façades became more grandiose and magnificent. Depending on the client's taste and the function of the building, they were built in the Neo-Romanesque, Neo-Gothic, Neo-Renaissance or Neo-Baroque style.

Historicism was found throughout Europe, but in Germany it tended to be both grander and more widespread. In 1871 the German Reich had at last been founded and the German nation reborn. The expectation of a general economic upturn led to hectic speculation, feverish building activity and a flood of new companies as the Germans worked vigorously to make up for what they thought they had missed in comparison to their neighbours. There were economic downturns, but people were earning more than ever before and this was evident in the costly and self-assertive style now called 'Wilhelmine' after the king of the time.

Around the turn of the century a reaction set in to the oppressive stucco and plush, and new forms of expression such as Jugendstil and, later, Expressionism, had some, limited impact on architectural styles. But by the start of the twentieth century architecture was determined by different impulses and aims. Technical progress and the demand for industrial building focused the attention of the avant-garde on industrial projects, and industrial design became a new discipline. Later the entire movement came to be called *Neues Bauen* (New Architecture) or *Neue Sachlichkeit* (New Objectivity), to describe the change of attitude towards form. Twentieth-century building was to be honest and, above all, it was to be without ornamentation or

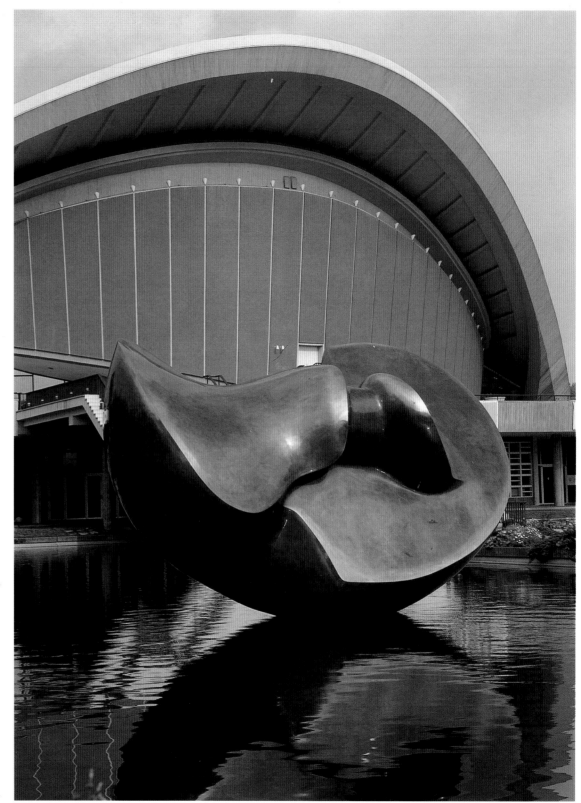

Left The Kongresshalle, or Congress Hall, in Berlin, which was the American contribution to the 1957 Building Exhibition. The dramatic curvilinear design is echoed by the similar, though more elaborate, shapes of Henry Moore's *Butterfly*, seemingly floating on the ornamental pool in front.

Right The Philharmonie concert hall in Berlin is the home of the Berlin Philharmonic Orchestra. The assymetrical tent-like structure was built in 1960–63 by H. Scharoun.

ostentation, with the structure derived rationally and logically from the function. It no longer needed to hide behind a façade. Some industrial buildings had been created in the new style before the First World War, like the AEG turbine factory building in Berlin by Peter Behrens and the Fagus works building in Alfeld by Walter Gropius.

The First World War broke into this mood of optimism, and for the Germans it brought a surprising and humiliating defeat. But despite the hunger, the economic crises and political chaos there miraculously emerged from the rubble and the moral and spiritual ruins a determination to build democratically for all classes according to the function and the needs of the time. That the new attitude developed and spread was mainly thanks to two centres of teaching and design, the Werkbund and the Bauhaus. The first was founded just before the First World War, and the Bauhaus just after, in 1919. In 1933 it was closed by the Nazis.

The concept for both organizations derived from the medieval *Bauhütten*, in which artists and craftsmen worked together without occupational or class distinction. Following that model the arts and crafts involved in building and furnishing a house as well as designing household equipment were united under one roof. This was felt to be the best way of planning and executing building projects in the present and the future. In these energetic and creative communities teachers and students, masters and apprentices exchanged ideas and experiences and discussed initiatives and enthusiasms. They felt bound by the common ideal of working towards formal goals that would combine functionalism with simplicity and clarity. Houses and their equipment, furniture and works of art were to be well built and within general financial means. As Walter Gropius, director of the Bauhaus, put it in 1923, 'We want to create a clear organic architecture, naked and radiant, following inner laws without playfulness or artificiality, which will affirm our environment of machines, wires and fast vehicles and which derives its meaning and purpose from itself through the tension between its own structures. These should be in a functional relationship to each other, and anything that can be dispensed with should be eliminated, as it would only blur the ultimate form of the building.'

In 1933 the National Socialists seized power in Germany. Their subsequent abuse of power was such that the grief and shame of this period can still stand in the way of an objective approach to German history. New Architecture was declared 'un-German' and its protagonists were persecuted, driven underground or abroad. They set up new schools in their host countries, and in Germany they left a gap that could only be filled after the National Socialists had been defeated and driven from power again.

Of the architecture of the Third Reich – fascist monumentalism expressing megalomaniac claims and ideas – it can only be said that just a small part of what was planned was implemented, and most of what was realized was destroyed again during the war. The Nazis drew on antiquity and Schinkel, but they perverted the Classical tradition with their colossal and oppressive structures. Although Albert Speer, Adolf Hitler's architect, wanted his buildings to stand, mighty and secure, for a thousand years, he actually incorporated the strangely morbid idea of their future destruction in them right from the start. Even their ruins were to be grandiose and proclaim the power and strength of the National Socialist movement.

A few years later, not only National Socialist buildings but many treasures of the past thousand years as well lay in ruins. The destruction brought upon Europe by the Germans had recoiled even more terribly upon their own country, and no-one saw any attraction any longer in a landscape of ruins. With

Two views of the Nationalgalerie in Berlin, a glass and steel structure built by Mies van der Rohe in 1962–8. With its glass walls it can be seen as an integral part of the modern city, both open to it (in the sense that its diverse nineteenth- and twentieth-century collection can be seen from outside) and reflecting its skyline.

dogged determination they were cleared away to make room for the reconstruction, a reconstruction that immediately raised crucial questions: should you rebuild in the old tradition, reconstruct the old buildings as if they had never been destroyed? Or should you seize the chance for a radical new beginning, unfettered by tradition? In the building boom of the 1950s many examples of both these approaches can be found; often, indeed, they are closely interlinked.

The post-war period has certainly brought less typically German architecture than earlier epochs. But unique buildings have emerged from the ruins, sometimes incorporating the remains of an old building in an exciting contrast to the new one, as in the Gedächtniskirche in Berlin or the Alte Pinakothek in Munich. The political situation of Germany differed considerably from other countries: when the Cold War split the world into two hostile camps, Germany was already divided in two, and the two German states maintained a hostile boycott of each other. Their architecture reflected their different economic systems. In the Eastern state building slowed down, although emergency restoration work

was carried out, but the West was caught up in what was almost an architectural over-reaction.

The Federal Republic of Germany embraced an 'international style', in which the ideas and controversies of the years before the war had been absorbed. Steel, glass and concrete, the new materials, perfected the skeletal way of building that had been pioneered centuries before by the timber-frame and Gothic builders. Only now the posts and supports were reinforced or pre-stressed concrete and steel wire, shaped or cast in rolling mills. Integrated designs for the ground plan and façades, in use since the nineteenth century to rationalize building, enabled buildings to shoot up.

In the international style cubist, functional structures based on the right angle had maintained their supremacy. During the 1950s this was supplemented by 'organic architecture', with asymmetrical curves and imaginative geometrical extravaganzas. In interior design the organic idea appeared in a more commonplace situation as the kidney-shaped table, while on roofs and walls it could intensify to such an extent that curved lines seemingly branched out into infinity. It was an appropriate form of expression for

an age when scientific progress had begun to make space travel possible.

With its dynamic form the organic house acquired the quality of a mobile organism. At the beginning of the 1960s the architect Hans Scharoun created in the Berlin Philharmonie a building whose multiple external walls are no longer at right angles to their foundations; they unfold, expand and seem to be swinging. Above them floats a spreading, asymmetrical roof. The Kongresshalle in Berlin also seemed in a witty way to be a living creature, trying to hold tight to its big round brim. The Berliners were quick to recognize the dynamic effect of the building and they nicknamed it the 'pregnant oyster', aptly a name with organic connotations.

In the examples mentioned so far the organic quality of the buildings was expressed by the shape of the building itself, and by the use of unorthodox angles and lines. But there are other ways of expressing this: organisms do not only move, they also interact with their environment, and that brings us to the second variant of organic architecture. Buildings with external walls made of glass both draw in their surroundings and extend out into them, while also reflecting the environment. Mies van der Rohe, a major exponent of this approach, created his new building for the Nationalgalerie in Berlin between 1962 and 1968, with a smooth, glass skin and a flat, projecting roof. The supports are internal and the structural skeleton is not visible. The view looking out is through curtain wall windows undefined by any stonework; there is a direct relationship with the world outside, while the viewer looking in sees the sky, light, clouds or the church of St Matthias opposite reflected in the glass.

The Federal Chancellor's Office in Bonn, built between 1969 and 1976, creates a dialogue with its environment in a different way. No building embodies the spirit of the old Federal Republic of Germany more than this. Three, almost exaggeratedly broad wings in glass, concrete and dark brown steel stretch over the grass beside the Rhine. The building is strikingly modern, except that it does not try to rise above two storeys. An office block humming with efficiency, it was built to display team work but not hierarchical divisions. With the two-storey arrangement of the core of the building, its glass skin and horizontal banding, the Federal Chancellor's Office nevertheless does not look like a glass palace, it is more like a cage with double bars.

Above The harsh rectangular outlines of the Bundeskanzleramt (Federal Chancellor's Office) in Bonn are seen through the voluptuous curves of Henry Moore's *Large Two Forms*.

Right The Palace of the Republic in East Berlin, with its wall of windows reflecting the Baroque Marstall building opposite.

Opposite The Kreishaus (Local Government Offices) in Siegburg, near Bonn, counterpointed by another piece of modern sculpture.

The building stands on supports, so that the ground and gardens seem to go right through the building. The intention was to let people walk under it while the work of government went on in the offices above, but such open access proved impossible to realize. In front of an inner courtyard stands Henry Moore's sculpture *Large Two Forms*, a compression of nature into organic shapes, like bones, skulls, shells or trees, which seem bent, broken and smoothed by endless movement.

The Palace of the Republic in East Berlin was built at the same time as the Federal Chancellor's Office in Bonn on the site of the Baroque Prussian palace. Designed to give the socialist state some importance and identity, it was built of concrete and gold-mirrored glass in the most modern and costly way possible. Opposite its south front the early Baroque Marstall building shimmers in the reflected light. With the Palace of the Republic the GDR also adopted the international style of architecture and used expensive materials to realize it. 'Just as in the West', said the people admiringly, a few words that embrace the motives, wishes and hopes of the two parts of Germany that are now setting about growing together again.

Left and below left The Neue Staatsgalerie in Stuttgart was built in 1984 by Sir James Stirling to house the city's collection of twentieth-century art. The strong lines and rich colours have been orchestrated to blend with the surrounding buildings.

Left The Züblin Building, on the southern outskirts of Stuttgart, is a recent office-building design (1983–4) by Professor Gottfried Bohm. One of the two seven-storey wings is seen here, with the central staircase on the right and one of the connecting walkways on the left, hung with leaves to soften its outlines. More plants provide a civilized ambience at ground level in the large space between the wings, which is spanned by a saddle-shaped glass roof and used for meetings and events.

Above The entrance courtyard of the Museum of Decorative Arts (1982–85) in Frankfurt am Main. Though in a modern idiom, it was designed to harmonize with the Neoclassical Metzler Villa, in whose grounds it was built (and which still houses part of the collection).

Left One of the striking spiral staircases in the wings of the Züblin Building. A crisp effect is achieved by the metal edges of the treads and the cool blue-grey colour scheme.

GARDENS

*Parks, gardens and courtyards throughout Germany
express both the spirit of the age and that of their creators,
ranging from the grand display of Sanssouci (opposite) to
the simple beauty of a window-box (above) on the tiled
façade of a traditional Saxon farmhouse.*

'The garden', as Bishop Hrabanus Maurus of Fulda, writing in the ninth century AD, began the garden chapter in his doctrinal poem on the world, 'is so called because plants are always growing there.' He was expressing the straightforward attitude of the early Middle Ages to its gardens. They were primarily intended to be of use, a place to grow medicinal plants and herbs. Each plant had seemingly to be sanctioned by a passage in the Bible; the Middle Ages was still far from planting gardens for pleasure or aesthetic enjoyment. The medieval garden was the opposite to the Garden of Eden, which God himself had created for mankind.

Later in the Middle Ages 'paradise' and *Minne* (love) gardens seem to have developed with many wild flowers in a still simple layout: a little fountain in the centre or a bank of lawn against a wall. Many had rose-covered pergolas or bowers, and most were under the windows of the ladies' quarters, so that the lady of the castle could look down from above on to a colourful carpet of flowers. The flowers grew haphazardly on the lawn, and the garden was usually entered through a narrow little gate. Our records of these gardens are mainly miniatures in handwritten manuscripts and books. The painters of the Middle Ages spoke through symbols and allusions, and flowers were a part of this symbolic language.

The Renaissance brought the Middle Ages to an end and marked the start of the early Modern Age. Italy rediscovered antiquity, a new feeling for life developed and the rest of Europe followed. Gardens underwent a particularly marked change at this time. With the new joy in life, in the earth and in man's likeness to God, who would want only a useful garden? From now on gardens were designed for pleasure and luxury. The new magnificence in Italy was the result of an early form of capitalism, as the Italian trade centres began to flourish. Tuscan and Roman merchant families rose to power, and they expressed their new wealth by building palaces and laying out gardens in the new style. To increase their standing and reputation they opened the gardens to interested travellers at certain times, as long as they observed the rules of behaviour, dressed properly and did not pick the flowers.

Italy was the model for Renaissance gardens, but Germany made something of her own out of them, as each traveller to Italy brought a different idea home with him. The originals were on the other side of the Alps and too far away for detailed observation;

Opposite The Baroque monastery near Freiburg im Breisgau. Germany's earliest gardens were in monastery courtyards and may have had a similar layout to this.

Right The garden of St Michael's monastery, Bamberg, has a symmetrical layout, with a star-shaped flowerbed surrounding a pool and fountain.

consequently, a surprising co-existence of the old and the new evolved in Germany. There were patrician gardens owned by proud citizens, richly planted gardens of scholars and botanists, and gardens for princely show, as in Munich and Heidelberg. Only the lesser nobility, in medieval castles, generally lacked the space for a Renaissance garden.

What did these new gardens look like? They reflected the new geocentric way of understanding the world, with man at its core. The Renaissance garden was orientated towards the centre, which was emphasized by a fountain, a sculpture or a little temple. The garden as a human creation meant organized variety in a limited space, and consequently its sections were clearly differentiated and symmetrically designed. Rare plants were eagerly cultivated, in tubs or vases, and exotic or decorative

birds like the peacock or pheasant were kept. Strong colours were preferred. The flowers, narcissi and hyacinths, fritillaria and irises, anemones and crocuses, were no longer strewn over the lawn but planted in straight rows and square beds. The tulip was brought from Asia Minor, and its many shades, in monochrome, flamed or marbled, created a firework display of colour in the beds. Growing tulips became fashionable, and bets were made as to which colour would evolve from the costly bulbs. Indeed, as the tulip fever grew the bulbs became a kind of currency.

One of the finest German Renaissance gardens to have survived, the Hofgarten in Munich (1613–17), was almost entirely enclosed by long arcades, nearly 600 metres (2000 ft) in length. It was this emphasis on enclosure that was changed by the French garden

designers of the next period, the Baroque. The dominating idea of this age was absolutism, which placed the king, as God's representative on earth, at the centre of a kind of terrestrial grid system. Hence the royal palace was always at the centre and at the junction of all routes by land or water. The central axis of the garden was given particular emphasis, and it was conceived as a necessary extension of the palace architecture into the outside world.

French garden design soon came to predominate all over Europe, and especially in Germany, where the new rules and principles were taken up with enthusiasm. Germany had just ended the exhausting Thirty Years' War. The tradition of garden design had been interrupted, the old masters were dead. This vacuum made the country susceptible to outside influence, but perhaps it was even more import-

Right The Great Garden at Herrenhausen, Hanover, the only German Baroque garden which has survived in its original form. A gigantic vase adorned with putti overlooks a typical pattern of formal flowerbeds fringed by statues. Formality and mathematical precision characterized gardens of this epoch, in contrast to the often exuberant style of Baroque buildings.

Opposite above Herrenhausen also boasts an open-air theatre, which is still used today for musical and theatrical productions. The flanking statuary is again orchestrated in a strictly formal way.

Opposite below The small Baroque garden at Schloss Belvedere, near Weimar, has a formal layout but on a much more intimate scale.

Pages 136–7 The spacious Rococo garden on the terrace below the east front of Schloss Augustusburg, Brühl, near Cologne, laid out by the French architect Francois Cuvilliés in 1728–40. The sinuous curves of the miniature hedges are interspersed with more formal pools and flowerbeds.

ant that when peace came the princes and electors began to vie with each other as to who was the brightest Sun King and who could produce the best copy of Versailles in his own small realm. But although they all imitated the same garden, about as many different versions resulted as Germany had states.

Outstanding in Germany is the Baroque garden at Herrenhausen (1665–6) in Hanover. It was initiated and inspired by one of the most percipient women on a throne in Germany, Princess Sophie. She was of English descent, from the House of Stuart, and mother to the future George I of England. Her letters are full of ideas and plans for her garden. She moved her personal rooms to the gallery, from where she could survey the work of planting, and she finally died in one of her parks. It is known that probably the most learned philosopher of the age, Gottfried Wilhelm Leibniz, who accompanied the princess on walks through the garden, influenced its design. It is, in fact, like a philosophical construction given tangible form. Shaped in a long rectangle, it is surrounded by straight canals and forms an absolutely geometrical ground plan. Involuntarily, the

Grosssedlitz, near Dresden, has an expansive Baroque layout based on Versailles. The formal pools and flowerbeds in front of the small country house give way to a series of broad descending terraces.

Opposite The orangery at the southern limit of the grounds of Schloss Weikersheim (Baden-Württemberg) has two wings which enclose a view down the Tauber valley and provide the alignment for the axis of the Baroque garden. The ornamental sculptures on the balustrades (unusually in sitting positions) represent Jupiter (left, foreground) and, on the right-hand wing, Mars, Apollo, Vulcan and Aeolus.

visitor is reminded of a chessboard or of well-functioning and skilfully constructed clockwork. No axes lead out into the landscape, and this heightens the absolute precision of all the parts.

The garden at Brühl, begun by Archbishop Clemens August of Cologne in 1728, followed the French pattern in that its central axis led far out into the landscape. The visitor can still stand on the southern terrace of Schloss Augustusburg at Brühl and look out over the bosquets, fountains and pools, following the hedges and rows of trees almost as far as another distant residence of the archbishop in Bonn. Unusually, the Brühl garden did not forget its medieval past: a long canal is laid around it like a moat and the old fortification has become decoration. Where a side avenue branches off lies one of the most entrancing hunting lodges of the time, Falkenlust.

Another variant of the French garden in Germany was the Zwinger in Dresden (1711–28). This served as a setting for the great festivities held by Augustus the Strong. It was like an outsize open-air banqueting hall, which brought together garden and gallery, amphitheatre and platform, lawn and stage, grotto and orange grove. It even continued Roman traditions, and seemingly you have to go back as far to find a comparable scale for the processions, jousts and tournaments, for the music and masquerades, and for the fountains and fireworks that took place. The greatest achievement of this opulent open air theatre was the inclusion of the river Elbe as a water axis to provide reflections, using the broad central vista down to the river. Seen from the Zwinger palace, the town is reflected in the river, the garden becomes the prelude to the landscape, and the steps leading down to the river act as a gondola harbour.

The play with landscape was intended to be even more dramatic at Wilhelmshöhe near Kassel. Water was to flood from the top of the forested hill down a steep set of steps to the foot of the palace. The most perfect Rococo ensemble in Germany, Sanssouci (1745–7) in Potsdam near Berlin, is based on the opposite movement. This summer residence stands at the top of a wonderfully curving hill, it is earthbound and yet elevated, while on one side the garden drops to a lower level in a series of six glass-covered terraces forming a kind of glazed vineyard.

In the last quarter of the eighteenth century, the first consistent expression of the Neoclassical movement on the continent of Europe was produced in the small Prussian state of Anhalt-Dessau. In the Elbe plains around his summer seat in Wörlitz Prince Leopold III, Frederick Franz of Anhalt-Dessau, created a kind of total work of art in the spirit of the Enlightenment. It also had the first landscaped garden on German soil. The prince had recently returned from a study tour in England and he laid out 'new parks' around his palace in the reserved and understated style of English country estates.

Avenues and pools, bridges and canals, parks and meadows, woods and buildings were grouped in a gentle and picturesque way, as if the landscape, with its bushes and trees, had grown naturally. The water was no longer symmetrically channelled into reflecting basins at geometrically significant points in the garden. In the Elbe plains the prince found a lake with a richly varied shape and numerous branches; he enlarged its bays, linking them with canals, and left the natural banks with their reeds, grass, ducks and loose, irregular clumps of trees.

The seemingly unhampered growth of the plants, the curving paths, the surprising glimpses of meadows and wooded hills, the play of uneven ground, all these natural elements in the park were enriched with ruins, Neoclassical temples, Neo-Gothic chapels and Chinese follies. Goethe called the ensemble the 'aesthetic garden', and he made the transition from the French garden to the English landscape park one of the themes of his novel

The stone bridge (1780) over one of the canals in the park of Schloss Ludwigslust in Mecklenburg-Western Pomerania. With its massive blocks and severe lines, the bridge is almost Neoclassical in style.

Right Small-scale circular temples, or monopteroi, were commonly used as garden ornaments during this period. This one at Hofgeismar, near Kassel, is by S. L. du Ry.

Wahlverwandtschaften (Elective Affinities). He also designed the Weimar park on the Ilm in the new 'aesthetic' style.

The English landscape gardens that were laid out everywhere at this time, as in Ludwigslust, for instance, met with some resistance in Germany. Friedrich Schiller commented on the German dilemma, caught between the French and the English tradition. The art of gardens, he said, had long followed architecture and its strict formality had had an oppressive effect on plant life.

> In more recent times garden architecture has retreated from that strange error, but only to lose itself in the opposite direction. Fleeing from the severe discipline of the architect it has taken refuge in the freedom of the poet, suddenly exchanging the hardest serfdom for the greatest licence, and now it wants to take its laws solely from the imagination.

Interestingly, the nineteenth century brought new ideas and the attempt to combine garden and landscape design with the industrial age that was then beginning. The start came with Friedrich Ludwig von Sckell, who after an apprenticeship in England became the most sought-after garden architect of his time. At Nymphenburg near Munich he left the Baroque parterre gardens next to the palace untouched, only laying out the outer areas of the park (1789–95) in the new English manner. But his visionary designs included more than the palace, the parks and the landscape. He used perspective so that the river, the Isar, formed a huge natural water axis, over which the city of Munich floated like a distant vision. It was a real image, and yet as a reflection it was also unreal, a playful symbolic allusion to the heavenly city of Jerusalem.

These ideas were taken up and embellished in Prussia. The architect Karl Friedrich Schinkel and the garden designer Peter Lenné were fortunate to serve the crown prince and later King Frederick William IV, who was passionately devoted to the visual arts, and they were able to work in a time of political calm after the upheavals of the Napoleonic wars and the Congress of Vienna. Under the prince's direction they transformed Berlin, Potsdam and the area in between into one of the most magnificent royal estates of the time, creating between 1825 and 1840 a 'Prussian Arcadia' in the style of the Italian Renaissance. It is fascinating to see how a Romantic programme was translated into landscape design on

the grand scale. The English ideas of the picturesque – blurring of axes and merging with the landscape – were combined with the strict French control of paths and water channels. The ideal landscape that was created here was not only to be beautiful but also modern and sensible. The cities, Potsdam and Berlin, were integrated meaningfully into nature, but at the same time agriculture, forestry and industry were coordinated and promoted. So beside fine classical buildings, hunting park, grounds, meadows and pastures rose smoking factory chimneys as symbols of progress.

In comparison with Lenné's progressive vision of garden design the great eccentric of German garden culture in the nineteenth century, Prince Pückler-Muskau, seems retrogressive. But his personality was too colourful to be overlooked. He was one of the richest landowners of his day, but his insatiable ambition for English landscaping totally ruined him. In agreement with his wife he obtained a legal divorce, in order to go to England and find a millionairess to marry. However, the plan did not succeed. But he did succeed in writing an account of his journey that proved a bestseller, and this almost restored his fortunes. Prince Pückler spent decades transforming his ancestral home in Muskau on the River Neisse into a total work of art. From the top of his hilly garden the garden landscape on both sides of the Neisse is visible; the town nestles in the valley and even the chimney of the chemical factory is a distant ornamentation. When the prince was financially ruined, he withdrew into a kind of late-Romantic aestheticism. In resignation he came to believe that the nobility were in any case doomed to destruction as a privileged class, and why then should he not, before departing, have the pleasure of an irrationally expensive, wonderful English garden? Prince Pückler's gardens in Muskau and Branitz are the finale to the great, private, English landscape gardens that were created in Germany.

You do not need to be a Prince Pückler to have a garden today. Since the First World War a house and a garden have no longer been the privilege of the upper or wealthy classes. The twentieth century, and especially the prosperity of West Germany, have brought together many different types of garden style, whether in the large municipal parks and public gardens, in villa and front gardens, or in farm and allotment, or 'Schreber', gardens. Window-boxes on house fronts are also prevalent throughout

The golden-lion fountain in the gardens in front of Schloss Kleinglienicke, Potsdam, built by K. F. Schinkel in 1824–6.

Germany but are a special feature of the south. You find them in many rural areas and in the villages and market squares where time seems to have stood still. Great, long boxes stand in front of wood-framed windows, displaying a wonderful cascade of summer flowers. No designer would dare to set such red tones next to each other or to mix white, yellow and blue together with such abandon. Window-boxes are often a substitute for front gardens, especially where streets are narrow and run right up alongside a house. A new feature is the popular 'eco-garden', where plants and small creatures can grow and live with and off each other without artificial fertilizers, pesticides or single cultures.

Widespread prosperity is evident in the design of gardens now. The further our fields and woods shrink and the more landscapes lose their natural outlines, the more time and effort are put into making ornamental gardens in new residential areas look beautiful and natural. The beds and flower beds are tastefully curved, and trees and bushes are placed in perspective, in the style of the old parks. Beech, birch and poplar, which can let their branches hang down like weeping willows, are particularly popular. Has the longing for the wide English park landscape found expression here on a smaller scale? The grudging can echo Oscar Wilde and call naturalness nothing but a pose. Those who are better disposed will be pleased with the peace and prosperity that have enabled this to happen and will appreciate all the care and attention that have gone into creating and maintaining these gardens.

Left These houses in the 'Little Venice' area of Wolfenbüttel, near Brunswick, back onto a canal, and the plants in their small garden enclosures and window-boxes seem to overflow into the water.

Far left Many of the tile-hung timber-framed houses in the villages of south-east Saxony have small but densely planted gardens which give a good show of colour even, as here, in late autumn. These are at Waltersdorf (above) and Obercunnersdorf (below).

Left A wine merchant's premises in Celle, Lower Saxony. The blue-painted doors make an attractive foil to the predominantly dark green foliage, with flowers adding touches of red, white and pink.

Left The typically colourful yard of another wine merchant's premises at Hambach, near Neustadt an der Weinstrasse, Rhineland-Palatinate. The profusion of plants helps to blend architecture of various ages and styles, including the arch in the foreground dated 1570.

Above Window-boxes and plants growing against a wall add to the colour scheme on the side of a village house in Tauberscheckenbach, Bavaria.

Left Overflowing window-boxes seem to turn a courtyard in Gengenbach, Baden-Württemberg, into a hanging garden.

Far left Red and white blooms provide an effective contrast to the pastel colours of the façades of houses in the Tanners' Quarter of Freiburg im Breisgau.

INTERIORS

*German interiors reflect a variety of cultural influences and
social classes, encompassing both the dramatic splendour
of a Baroque staircase (opposite) at Schloss Weissenstein
ob Pommersfelden and the rustic charm of an old
farmhouse entrance hall (above) in Saxony.*

Burg Eltz

RHINELAND-PALATINATE

When Germans are asked to name the best place to visit in their country many say Burg Eltz, for it is the quintessence of German medieval Romanticism. Its picturesque position is as impressive as its coherence and unity. Burg Eltz provides one of the few surviving records of the daily life of a single family over 800 years. A fortress and a residence, it stands proudly on a steep rock in the deeply cleft ravine of the Eltzbach valley, above the town of Moselkern and its vineyards, and it is one of the few castles that are fortunate enough never to have been destroyed. Only a fire in 1920 has caused some damage, which was

Above Burg Eltz is best seen from above in the early morning when a mist often rises from the valley below.

Left The courtyard buildings manage to combine styles from a number of different periods in a harmonious way. These were the living quarters which used to house up to a hundred members of the family and some of them are still living there today.

Above The Elector's Room has four fine Rococo chairs which date from the early eighteenth century and are probably of Flemish origin, while the Belgian tapestry in the background dates from around 1680 and depicts the start of an autumn hunting expedition.

Left The Hall of Banners has a late Gothic star-ribbed vault such as was only found in the noblest living quarters. The tiled stove in the corner is a so-called 'Evangelists' Stove' because it shows the authors of the four gospels. It was heated from the kitchen next door.

Below The wall paintings in the dressing room date from the late Gothic period.

repaired. It is immediately clear that this angular structure was built not for comfort but for security; it is so narrow and has such high walls. What this steep hill in the narrow Eltz valley could not provide in the way of space, the builders sought to produce by projecting their slender half-timbered towers up into the sky.

Burg Eltz enters recorded history in 1137, when Rudolf von Eltz acknowledged the gift from the Emperor Frederick Barbarossa. At that time feudalism was just evolving and with it the castles and residences whose indestructible walls were to form the military basis of the lord's power.

Since the first Rudolf von Eltz an unbroken succession of barons and counts have borne the same name and inhabited the castle. They formed a *Ganerbenburg*, a community of heirs in which several lines of the same family are linked. All the descendants of the head of the family lived together and inherited jointly, settling the use of the castle and the distribution of obligations and rights between them by agreement. By the thirteenth century the family had divided into three branches, and they each added a supplement to the common family name to distinguish between them. Like the castle itself the names of these branches – Golden Lion, Silver Lion and Buffalo Horn – recall the magic of the Middle Ages and its fairytale world. At times more than 120 members of the family have lived together in the castle.

In the Middle Ages each individual branch of the family had its own wing in the castle and this is what makes the complex as a whole so picturesque. Its architectural high point is the inner courtyard, where the variety of the building can be seen most clearly. A product both of nature and man, Burg Eltz is a monumental witness to a time in which a family had to rely on itself and its powers of self-defence. Today's visitor can trace the stages of civilization itself – first the early period, when the needs of defence behind high walls predominated, and then a later period, when the decorative refurbishment of the rooms became possible. In nearly all of them the historical inventory has survived and the domestic culture of earlier centuries can be seen. This family has been able to adapt flexibly to changing times, and in their castle they have managed to preserve an impressive historical and artistic treasure.

Above The loft dates from the late fifteenth century.

Right An open-fronted wall cupboard in the kitchen contains vessels for a variety of uses.

Schloss Mespelbrunn

BAVARIA

Germany's wildest and most famous robber tale is set in the Spessart hills. The story tells of ambushed post coaches, helpless countesses, and a dark and gloomy inn in the depths of the forest. There is a sinister and evil robber chief and rescue comes only at the very last minute. In the middle of this part of the forest there was a remote clearing beside a lake which was called 'Zum Espelborn'. This Archbishop Johann of Mainz gave to the Knight Hamann Echter of the Odenwald on 1 May 1412 in thanks for loyal service against Czech aggressors. Schloss Mespelbrunn reflects the troubled times in which it was built. It was a solid fortress with heavy walls and towers, tiny arched windows cut into the thick walls and elongated slits in the keep, from which the soldiers could shoot. In the sixteenth century, when times were calmer again in Germany, Mespelbrunn also changed. The old moated fortress was greatly extended and made into a Renaissance house, and since then stepped gables have adorned the façades and softened its stern appearance. The interior courtyard acquired arcades, columns and a portal – typical early Renaissance architectural forms from Upper Italy – but they were applied with such abandon and so asymmetrically that little of the Italian harmony has remained. However, the sixteenth-century builders did create a residence that was rooted in local traditions, full of life and close to the people, a fine example of how the German Renaissance absorbed Italian influence and of how the old Gothic style was linked with the new to create an individual piece of architecture.

As the years went by, the interior was also furnished more richly and elaborately. Painters and stucco artists decorated the walls, and the official rooms were filled with works of art of high quality: paintings, tapestries, furniture and porcelain. In the nineteenth century, when interest and taste in Germany turned back to the medieval past under the influence of the Romantic movement, Mespelbrunn was loved as one of the country's greatest treasures. It entered literature and became the subject of sonnets and the scene of novels and tales. The building also underwent changes according to the spirit of the times. The fairytale qualities of the moated castle were emphasized: the courtyard,

Below The courtyard with its arcades and columns shows the influence of the Italian Renaissance style.

Above and left The moated Renaissance house of Mespelbrunn named after 'Zum Espelborn', a remote glade beside a lake where the original fortress was built.

closed until then, was opened to the lake with a picturesque arch. The façade looking onto the water was given a romantic oriel window and an arcade, charming and simple testimonies to the nineteenth-century longing for the lost paradise of the Middle Ages.

Perhaps Schloss Mespelbrunn can move the visitor today even more than in earlier times. The intimacy of the place, which has been in private ownership since it was built, has not been reduced in any way by its popularity. Anyone who has walked through the dense forest of the Spessart and entered the quiet courtyard, with the ivy-covered arcade, the round towers, the warm red sandstone pillars and the coats of arms and reliefs on the façade, will feel enveloped in an atmosphere that has survived through all the centuries, untroubled by fire, siege, war or decay.

Right A grotesque self-portrait of the architect on one of the arches in the courtyard. The outsize head may have been intended to reflect his superior intelligence, and symbolically he appears to be carrying the building for which he was responsible on his shoulders.

Below Door in the courtyard, leading to the staircase. The sculpted figures above the door show the builder and his wife, and appear to have been added five years after the door was built in 1564.

Below A typical wood-burning stove in the Ancestors' Hall is unusually supported by complete figures of lions rather than their feet alone.

A corner of the Ancestors' Hall, which is dominated by a magnificent Italian cabinet with an unusual metal inlay creating a perspective view.

Schloss Küps

BAVARIA

Of all German castles, Schloss Küps seems a particularly good example of Bertolt Brecht's 'Mother Courage'. Since it was built in the Middle Ages it has always been at the centre of events. It has profited from the changing times and suffered under them, withstood storms and granted protection.

Küps came into the possession of the imperial Barons von Redwitz at the beginning of the thirteenth century, but by the end of the Thirty Years' War in 1648 it lay in ruins. Reconstruction started in 1660, as in many places throughout the Reich. The mighty, early medieval walls of the old structure were used as foundations and the new Baroque residence was built on top of them. Wall strength proved a particular problem, but the builders made a virtue of necessity and put the state rooms on the second floor – an particularly but flexible solution. The rooms on the first and second floors of the new palace were decorated by the distinguished Vogel family, so Küps has particularly valuable polychrome stucco ceilings. These were repainted several times in the past century and have only recently been restored to their original pastel delicacy.

On the ground floor of the residence a large chapel was erected. This was important at Küps because the Barons von Redwitz had remained Catholic after the end of the Thirty Years' War and had allowed the Catholic faithful from the surrounding villages to attend mass in their chapel, even though the local community, which was under the patronage of the

Left and below The *Jagdsaal* (hunting room) on the second floor derives its name from the birds and hunting scenes portrayed in the stucco decoration on the ceiling. In the alcove (left) an ancient Cypriot vase stands under one of the windows.

Far left The main façade of Küps overlooking the courtyard. Küps boasts the first mansard roof to be built in Germany, after the original owners saw them at Versailles.

Right A corner of the sitting room with the more formal staircase landing beyond.

Below right Detail of the Music Room ceiling.

lord of the estate, had become Protestant. That they were still the patrons of the local Protestant church community shows how strong the human bonds were between the castle and the village. It is evidence that tolerance could still be practised in the land, although it was exhausted by the religious wars.

The residence has always been in the hands of the same family. All the modernization work to park and house has been done so carefully that nothing essential has been altered. Changing economic conditions this century made it necessary to break up the farm and sell off forest and fields, and since then the estate has no longer been the basis of the family's income. During the Second World War the owner fell at the front without an heir, and the female line inherited; some of the old furniture was also lost when the war broke out. At the end of the war sixty refugees from the east were quartered in the house and lived in Küps for twenty years. It has now been divided into ten flats and has been refurbished in a personal and tasteful way. As the photographs show, Küps has well withstood the trials and tribulations of the twentieth century.

Above The windows and pilasters on the garden front of this residence in Baden-Württemberg echo the entrance façade. The garden is distinguished by an impressive collection of Baroque statuary.

Above left The entrance front is dominated by massive red sandstone pilasters.

Left Coaches and horses used to pass through this great hall in a house which is still a family home today.

Right Dark hunting trophies contrast with the light cross-vaulted ceiling of the staircase leading from the great hall to the principal living rooms above.

A Baroque Residence

BADEN-WÜRTTEMBERG

The family whose residence is shown here came from Austrian ancestral lands in the sixteenth century and were in the service of the Elector Prince of the Palatinate when the War of the Palatinate Succession broke out in 1688. In acknowledgement for the special services he had rendered during the hostilities the forebear to whom the family owe their ascendancy was given the title of *Reichsgraf* (count) by the elector as well as some land on the edge of the Odenwald. His son also achieved high rank, which required an imposing residence.

The son built the family seat between 1710 and 1720, and its debt to the palaces of Upper Italy is very evident. On the main façade of the three-storey, single-wing building a colossal pilaster order rises above the entrance. The pilasters are in red sandstone and stretch up to the roof. The really original architectural feature was a huge stone cupola with numerous windows that once towered over the great main hall of the residence. It is, however, no longer to be seen, for to the annoyance of the count it caused intractable structural problems right from the start, and after seemingly endless repair work it had to be removed because it was likely to bring the whole house down.

What has remained is a simple rectangular structure, whose particular charm owes something to this curious architectural history. The great hall, which lay under the former dome and has remained at the centre of the house, occupies nearly a quarter of the entire building and was originally intended as a passage for coaches and horses. The floor, columns and stairs are in elegant red sandstone.

The hall is a telling illustration of the problems that owners of old palaces and castles face in the twentieth century. This architecture was for show; it was intended to proclaim the power and dignity of the owner and his sovereign and to demonstrate taste and an understanding for art. Today these residences have to serve as a focus for a family, and it is not easy to find the right balance between beauty and historical heritage, comfort and practical economy. In all its aspects – gardens, external structure and interior decoration – this Baroque residence shows that at the end of the twentieth century culture, tradition, taste and family pride can be combined.

Left A gleaming brass door sets off the white ceramic tiles of this stove in a corner of the Yellow Saloon.

Opposite above The state rooms on the first floor have contrasting colour schemes although they share the same magnificent parquet floor.

Opposite below The small family sitting room on the ground floor has a rare example of a spiral staircase, which leads to the state rooms above.

Below The attractive and modest-sized dining room is in everyday use by the owners.

Left The mood of the library is set by the mellow, oak bookcases and doors, while the red velvet upholstery of the chairs is complemented by blue walls.

A Baroque Country House

HESSE

Towards the end of the great era of building activity in the eighteenth century this country seat was built in Odenwald, a region containing a great many fine German palaces. In many respects the new building was a typical German family seat. The many small houses built by the nobility during these years could not match the great residences, but they often achieved an artistic rank that underlined the aristocracy's position as the élite of the land.

Towards the end of the eighteenth century the influence of the Italian villa became more apparent. This house also looks forward to the emergence of Neoclassicism, although the Baroque tradition still predominates. Built in 1771, the house is a stately structure with a mansard roof and projecting central sections on both the long and short sides. Elegant and imposing, it was a status symbol for the imperial and local rulers. The landowner was well equipped for his task as builder. After studying at the Cathedral School in Würzburg and then in Mainz and Leipzig, he had been sent on the Grand Tour, which was essential for all the young nobles in Europe at the time, to enrich his knowledge of architecture and the fine arts and perfect his manners.

He entered the service of the territory's ruler, Johann Friedrich, Archbishop of Mainz, and his career prospered. He began as court councillor to the archbishop, rose to be a privy councillor, then bailiff, lord marshall, lord high chamberlain and finally imperial and royal chamberlain. His magnificent residence testifies to the importance of his many positions and the success he enjoyed in his career. He was even able to obtain the services of an architect of the quality of Johann Leonard Stahl for his work. Stahl had been taught by Balthasar Neumann and

Left The central section of the south aspect of the house which was formerly the entrance front.

Opposite The former stables, which are an architectural reflection in miniature of the main house.

Left The marble fireplace in the drawing room. Central heating radiators are cleverly concealed behind the metal grills at the sides.

Above right The Great Saloon on the first floor is mainly used for entertaining. The walls are covered in light blue silk which complements the upholstery and makes a pleasing contrast to the rich grain of the wooden floor.

Below Detail of the floor in the Great Saloon, which was made from door panels brought from the family's town house in Worms.

was under contract to the Elector Prince von Schönborn, but he was able to work on this house as well as the Schönborn's residence at Bruchsal.

The house was originally only a summer seat, and in the winter months the family lived in various town houses in the Rhineland. However, the Rhineland was soon to be occupied and devastated by the French revolutionary army, so the summer seat, on the other bank of the Rhine, became a place of refuge where the imperial and royal chamberlain spent the entire year. The situation hardly improved in the next century, and at times the house had to be rented out. But when the family regained full possession of

it, in the middle of the nineteenth century, they were able to restore its old dignity and brilliance, only making renovations in the original Baroque style.

Since then the house has continued to be the family's home, and the present generation has set its own stamp on it. Traditions are kept alive, but the house and garden are not only being maintained, they are also being adapted to modern living conditions. The smoking room, formerly the place where the gentlemen would retire to talk undisturbed over cognac and cigars after dinner, is now the place where the whole family meet. The house shows that old and new can be combined with taste and understanding.

Above Dark wood and delicate Rococo ornamentation are used for the walls and doors in the billiard room.

Left Refreshingly bright decor characterizes the dining room much used by the family today.

Schloss Weissenstein ob Pommersfelden

BAVARIA

Anyone travelling down the old road along the river Main from Bayreuth to Frankfurt is literally travelling across the centre of Europe. The road also forms the central axis in Germany, separating north from south. It used to separate the northern might of Protestant Prussia from the Catholic Hapsburgs in the south. For a long time the Schönborn dynasty ruled in this area. They were an old Rhenish family and during their reign of two hundred years they provided many of the outstanding Prince Bishops of Bamberg and Würzburg, Archbishops of Mainz, Elector Princes and Chancellors of the Reich. Pos-

terity has almost forgotten the political role played by the Schönborns, but the family has made itself immortal as builders, with the many generously planned, innovative and stately buildings, such as palaces, churches, stables, administration buildings, stores and residences, that were scattered all over the areas under their sway.

Lothar Franz von Schönborn, who built Schloss Weissenstein ob Pommersfelden between 1711 and 1718, was Elector Prince Archbishop of Mainz and Prince Bishop of Bamberg, and so one of the ecclesiastical rulers whose worldly power was only ended by secularization in 1803. He was devoted to architecture and painting, had travelled far in his youth and visited many palaces and galleries. Schloss Weissenstein, near the village of Pommersfelden,

Above Designed by the Elector Lothar Franz von Schönborn, the palace of Schloss Weissenstein (1711–18) near the village of Pommersfelden is a supreme example of German Baroque at its most magnificent. The elector's court architect, Johann Dientzenhofer, was responsible for the façade.

Right The vaulted and richly decorated Garden Room was designed by Georg Hennicke as a grotto. Because of its coolness and freshness it was often used by the elector and his court in the summer.

Opposite The grand staircase occupies the entire central section of the house. Ascending in two flights to the main floor, the stairs offer constantly changing views and perspectives, and the balustrade is decorated with highly elaborate pieces of sculpture like the urn (right) in the staircase hall.

was his own personal home, not an official residence, and is still in the family's possession today. Originally the old moated castle in the village itself was to be renovated and extended, but then the prince bishop decided against schemes that seemed to force compromises on him. Brooding at night over the plans, he himself drew the design for one of the greatest Baroque buildings and the first great palace building of the eighteenth century on German soil.

Schloss Weissenstein has an 'E'-shaped ground plan with pavilions at each corner. The main wing has a great central section which projects far into the *cour d'honneur*; this gives the building the sense of movement as well as ceremonial monumentality that are so characteristic of Baroque architecture, while the long, flatter garden front radiates calm and peace. The heart of the central section is the grand staircase, and it is one of the greatest and boldest Baroque creations. The prince bishop himself appears to have played a decisive part in its design. The huge dimensions of the space are evident to the visitor as soon as he enters. The stairs ascend in two flights to the main storey, offering changing views and perspectives at every step. A triumphant ceiling fresco spans the whole hall like the heavens themselves and amusingly (in a Christian archbishop's house) includes the pre-Christian gods of Olympus.

Left The stucco ceiling in the Cabinet of Mirrors. The blue background may have been intended to represent the cosmos.

Above Part of the metalwork covering one of the doors in the Cabinet of Mirrors.

Left A corner of one of the mirrors in the same room, which typically had the secondary purpose of displaying porcelain.

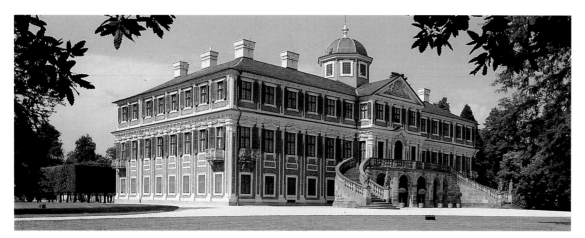

Schloss Favorite

BADEN-WÜRTTEMBERG

The Margrave Ludwig Wilhelm von Baden, Field Marshall of the Reich and Imperial General, had won such distinction in the Turkish wars that he was nicknamed 'Turkish Louis', and although a rough, aggressive ruler, he was also smitten by another great passion of his time, building. When he died in 1707, he left a young wife, Sibylle Augusta von Sachsen-Lauenburg, and several small children.

The margravine, who governed his estate in Rastatt for the next twenty years, had lent strong support to her husband in all his building projects. Shortly after his death she decided to build a palace and a pleasure garden with a hundred fountains in nearby woods between Rastatt and Baden-Baden, where she could withdraw into solitude and tranquillity and rest from the business of government. In the brilliant and exquisite architecture of Favorite she created a unique testimony to the age of Baroque, and it has come down to us, carefully maintained and untouched by war.

Posterity has assumed that the margravine led an extravagant life in Schloss Favorite, presumably because she had the words 'Pray for the great sinner' carved on her gravestone. But this is so typical of the time that the margravine can be exonerated. The contradictions of the double life which the margravine led in her pleasure palace were also typical of the time. With its gardens and all the extravagant luxury of the interior, it served her for enjoyment, for festivities and masked balls, but she still liked to withdraw there to pray and repent. She would chastise herself in the Chapel of St Mary Magdalen in the park, to obtain spiritual purification, or eat a bowl of cold porridge by candlelight in the small dining salon, surrounded only by life-size wax figures of the Holy Family.

The margravine proved an energetic and skilful ruler, and she was passionately devoted to the arts. Her soldier husband had been obsessed by architecture, but she built in order to provide the right setting for her collections of *objets d'art* and crafts. This is evident from the external form of the building, which is a strange mixture: too small for a great palace and too sophisticated for a retreat. The northern façade is dominated by the projecting stairway and central section, in the pediment above which float putti, holding the coat of arms of the Baden-Lauenburg alliance. All the outside walls are faced with granite fragments and pebbledash, which children in the surrounding villages eagerly collected and sold to the margravine. They lend the building a highly original and lively appearance, which is further underlined by the red sandstone sculptures on the sides of the stairs.

The interior is the most exciting and characteristic aspect of the building. Every room is like a curio cabinet, a miniature cosmos, in which curiosities and extraordinary works of art and crafts have been collected and displayed. The aesthetic pleasure these offer is intensified by optical illusions, broken perspectives and arbitrary reflections. From object to object, from picture to image and counter-image, the delight in earthly things has become so fantastic and irrational that the references to the transience of life and to death found everywhere seem to develop naturally and consistently from it.

Above The stove in the corner of the family room is covered with blue-painted faïence tiles.

Left The 'Sala Terrena', around which the palace is built, rises the full height of the building and looks onto the garden. The blue tiles were made at Nuremberg in imitation of delftware.

Opposite The main façade of Schloss Favorite has a strong central focus with its two flights of steps and balustrades leading up to a projecting centre section, which is surmounted by a highly decorated pediment and topped by an octagonal cupola.

Left The Mirror Room contains over 300 looking glasses at every conceivable angle to the walls and ceiling. The multiple, distracting reflections they create exemplify the Baroque taste for the fantastical and irrational.

Below far left Detail of the polished marble floor in the Audience Chamber.

Below left A wall panel in the Florentine Room. Painted papier mâché has been combined with silk flowers.

The Florentine Room contains a complete fantasia of images – miniature portraits, figures, landscapes, flowers, birds and beasts executed in a variety of artistic media – which cover the walls, ceiling and floor. Centrally located on each wall is a mirror overlaid with a gilt trellis.

Right The north, garden front of the moated Schloss Schwarzenraben. It is more like a Bavarian palace than a conventional Westphalian country seat.

Below The entrance in the *cour d'honneur* is marked by an elegant twin flight of stairs.

Schloss Schwarzenraben

NORTH RHINE-WESTPHALIA

Not far from the scene of the Niebelungenlied, in one of the oldest cultivated landscapes in Germany, lies the magnificent, moated Baroque palace of Schwarzenraben. It stands amid flat fields, pollarded willows and avenues of poplars, where the Westphalian plain is threaded by rivers winding towards the Lower Rhine. The palace was built in the second half of the eighteenth century, and today it is owned by an old Westphalian family, the Barons von Ketteler. As was usual in Westphalia, the building stands on oaken pillars hammered at least 4 metres (13 ft) down into the boggy ground and is surrounded by a moat.

This is a dream palace, of exquisite beauty and not so large as to be overpowering. It has outhouses, a farm, a park, a fine orangery, a *cour d'honneur* and escutcheons. What at first looks like perfect Baroque symmetry on a more careful examination reveals minor discrepancies, showing that many generations

Right The chapel was the last room in the house to be finished, in 1777. The figures on the altar, though by the local artist Josef Stratmann, are very Bavarian in character and it is thought that Stratmann spent some time there as a young man.

have lived here and helped to shape the place. Outwardly, the building is quietly elegant. Many rooms inside, on the other hand, contain ecstatic examples of Rococo decoration in white and gold, complicated and light at once, especially the jewel-like chapel, where the owners pray in a small enclosure on elegant Louis XVI chairs. All this lifts Schwarzenraben far above its provincial setting.

The Barons von Hörde, who owned the estate in the sixteenth century, called it *Schwarzenraben*, the 'Black Raven'. No-one knows why, but the name is romantic enough to have given rise to legends. One says that a raven showed this place to wandering monks in the ninth century, when they were taking a relict to the monastery of Corvey. Another is that the first bird to settle on the roof of the Baroque palace when it was finished in 1778 was a raven, and this gave the palace its name.

The palace itself has given rise to speculation. Was it not very much more costly and luxurious than a country estate could support? A more modest residence did formerly stand here, and at the beginning of the eighteenth century it was only intended to enlarge it slightly. But then a talented and hard-working Baron von Hörde advanced surprisingly rapidly in the service of the Archbishop and Elector of Cologne, Clemens August. He rose to the much-envied and well-paid position of bailiff in the archbishopric of Cologne. There were presumably particular reasons for the ruler's favour. In June 1736 the archbishop, who was a passionate hunter, had come to Schwarzenraben with a hunting party, but in the eagerness of the chase he had the misfortune to shoot his noble host in the leg. It was worse than an accident, it was a blunder that had to be handled discreetly and made good in an elegant way. That is probably why the baron was heaped with rich offices, making the construction of a fitting residence not only possible but necessary.

As an official or bailiff Baron von Hörde had to be the mirror of his ruler, publicly and privately, and Clemens August was a Wittelsbacher, that is, a Bavarian prince. He was a friend of France, art-loving and ostentatious. He was just embarking upon his transformation of the Rhineland in Bonn, Brühl and Cologne into a Baroque wonderland, and so Schwarzenraben was endowed with the magic of French Baroque architecture and the elegance of a Munich town palace, cut down to Westphalian proportions.

Left The Stucco Room on the ground floor provides outstanding examples of the magnificent Rococo decoration to be found in the house.

Far left A corner of the dining room, also on the ground floor, with a cast-iron stove which dates from around 1800.

Right The entrance hall, where an overzealous painter seems to have included the doors in his marbling work although they would never have been made of marble.

Left The Small Saloon. The fresco in the corner dating from about 1780 depicts imperial and Turkish tents and is intended to represent the camp where the Hapsburg and Turkish embassies met for negotiations.

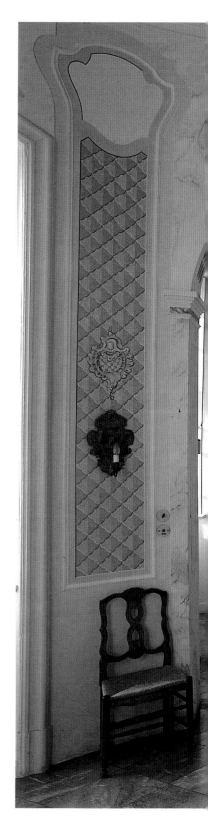

Schloss Nassau

RHINELAND-PALATINATE

On its way to the Rhine the River Lahn winds through narrow valleys, past the forested Taunus and Westerwald and then past the old town of Nassau. On its banks are picturesque castles and ruins, and many of them have belonged to the Counts of Nassau, whose female line still occupies European thrones today. One of the castles in Nassau, however, was inhabited by the Barons vom Stein. In the seventeenth century, when castles had really lost their military importance, the family moved to the other bank of the river and into the town. Here they extended their residence, a simple late Renaissance building, into an imposing home with a square stair tower, later adding side wings. Thus arose a country seat of quiet beauty, which was typical of the German

The decoration of the library (right) with its warm-coloured wooden panelling contrasts with the elegant blue decor of the adjacent dining room (below).

Above The original medieval structure of Schloss Nassau was enlarged in the early seventeenth century to form a Renaissance house with a staircase tower, which can be seen on the right. On the left is the Neo-Gothic tower added by Baron vom Stein in 1814–18.

cultural tradition where the family lived in the provinces but were always at the forefront of the intellectual and artistic life of their time.

The last member of the vom Stein family, which thereafter continued in the female line, was its most famous. Born in Nassau in 1757, Baron Heinrich vom Stein became a Prussian minister and reformer and a passionate opponent of Napoleon. He was a new type of politician, neither soldier nor courtier but a civilian administrator in the Prussian government when the state was in one of its deepest crises: the Prussian armies had been annihilated in 1806 at Jena and Auerstedt by Napoleon, the state had proved incapable of defending itself and the people were by and large uninvolved in government. In the famous Nassau memorandum of 1807 the baron reasoned that if the people were kept away from any

involvement in the state, the state could not count on them in its hour of need and demand their support. Stein's plans for reform therefore involved ending absolutism in Prussia and making it a constitutional state, in which each person would play an active part and feel bound to it.

The reforms remained fragmentary, because Baron vom Stein was dismissed from his ministerial post after a year. That was tragic for Prussia and for Germany, but it was beneficial for Nassau, to which he returned. In 1814 he added a singular structure to his palace. The Prussian people had by now obtained their freedom from Napoleon in the Wars of Liberation, and the French emperor had experienced 'God's judgement', as vom Stein called it, at the Battle of the Nations near Leipzig. As a memorial to this he had a three-storey Neo-Gothic tower built to

an octagonal ground plan. He put a study on the first floor, while the third floor contains the memorial hall for the Wars of Liberation, with marble busts of the rulers of the three allied powers, Franz II of Austria, Frederick William III of Prussia and Alexander I of Russia.

The baron was a great admirer of the romantic Neo-Gothic movement, which in Germany after the Napoleonic Wars had little in common with the 'charming, venerable Gothick' of Horace Walpole. The German enthusiasm for the medieval past and the *altteutscher Styl* was bound up with ideas of national German regeneration. But the Nassau tower today reminds the visitor not so much of the Wars of Liberation as of the statesman who spent all his energy in the provinces because he was prevented from carrying out his great reforms.

Above and above left The study on the first floor of the Neo-Gothic tower. The octagonal room has a vaulted ceiling whose arches enclose portraits of German historical figures, while the detail (above left) shows how books are kept between the wooden panelling and the outer wall.

Above The Liberation Hall on the top storey of the Neo-Gothic tower was the first of its kind to be built to commemorate the defeat of Napoleon.

Left The entrance door to the Neo-Gothic tower, often called Schinkel's Tower, although he was not the architect, but the design was influenced by his work.

Left This typical Black Forest farmhouse with its projecting roof, wooden structure and stone foundations has remained basically unchanged for centuries.

Below The former bedroom, which would have been warmed by the adjacent kitchen and living room, is today a sitting room.

An Old Farmhouse in the Black Forest

BADEN-WÜRTTEMBERG

In the upper Black Forest lies a village whose houses are scattered around a high valley, although it is evident that they belong together. They are all built in the same style and are set against a background of sloping hills, with meadows and pastures stretching behind them. Higher up, the pasture changes to forest.

At a height of 900 metres (3000 ft) the climate is harsh. Crop farming was never very rewarding here, but the slopes offer ideal pasture land. For centuries the calves and young oxen have been driven up to the higher pastures in the early summer, where they stay until the autumn, while the dairy cows graze on the lower slopes and are brought home for milking in the evening. But for most of the year the livestock are in their stalls and need an enormous amount of hay. That is why farmhouses like this one have space for a huge hay loft under their high roof. To fill it every inch of ground around the houses and the whole village is used to grow hay.

This farm was first mentioned in documents in 1711 as a single-family farmhouse, and that was certainly the year in which it was built. On the eastern side, protected from the wind, was the

The loft under the high-pitched roof now houses the owner's collection of *objets d'art* from various parts of the world, including Kilim rugs from East Anatolia, ostrich eggs from Somalia and an Indian sitar.

The living room retains many features typical to this part of the Black Forest, with at one end a large tiled stove (right), which was the focus and the source of warmth for the whole house. The stone bench with its wooden pillow was the place where the elderly and ill could rest, while the stove itself was employed for baking bread and keeping food hot as well as for heating the sacks of cherry stones used to warm the beds. At the other end of the room (opposite), above and to the left of the table and chairs, is a tiny vessel for holy water with a cross above it.

entrance to the two-storey living area, while the farm facilities were on the ground floor. It had a feeding passage, from which the hay was shovelled into the nearby stalls. Above this, on the south side of the house, lay the threshing floor. It was open to the roof, which, built to what was then the latest development in carpentry, sits on its rafters like a stool on sloping legs.

Like all typical Black Forest farmhouses, there is a ramp up which hay-waggons could drive to the raised threshing floor. The huge hay loft was beside this, on the same raised level and protected by the same timber roof. The most characteristic feature of Black Forest farmhouses is the projecting roof, designed to protect the house from wind, snow and rain on the weather sides, north and west, but on the south and east sides it only stretches a little way beyond the façade, so that the rays of the sun can reach the house.

Apart from the foundations of stones and mortar, the house was entirely made of wood, including an outer cladding of shingles, for in the surrounding woods fir and pine were readily available. The farmers generally worked as carpenters to add to their meagre earnings from the infertile farm land, and each would make the wooden shingles for his own house. Here rounded shingles are nailed in overlapping diagonal rows so that the surface beneath is covered more than once. Up to the twentieth century the big roof was also shingled, but today it has a dark grey roof of 'Eternit' slates. With the years they will acquire a light grey patina and in colour at least will begin to look like the old, darkened shingles.

An Umgebindehaus

SAXONY

Linen production and trade had been a source of wealth in the Lausitz area of Saxony since the Middle Ages. It was also connected with a particular local feature, the *Umgebindehäuser*, or 'buttressed houses', a manner of building that later spread from Saxony into Bohemia and Silesia. The finest of these houses belonged to the factors, or middlemen, former weavers grown rich by buying the thread and taking it to the cottage-weavers, who then had to hand back the finished cloth to the factors. Unlike their counterparts in Silesia and Westphalia, the Saxon factors did not adopt an urban culture with their growing wealth. Full of brightly painted furniture and other embellishments, their homes were more elaborate, richer and more cultivated than other local dwellings, but they remained genuine farmhouses.

The house shown here is a particularly fine example of its kind, typical of the local architecture in Oberlausitz, where Slav and Germanic traditions have mingled in the border area, and fortunately still in its original condition. The structure might be called a synthesis between a log cabin and a timber-framed construction, but basically it is a technically highly skilful way of binding together the horizontal and vertical stresses of a building. The great structural problem for houses built with a skeleton frame is that the ground floor – and in these houses it consists of a single large room – is unable to carry the load of the upper floor and roof. For this reason the weight was taken off the load-bearing walls by supporting them from the outside with wooden posts joined together as arcades. These were freely visible and often carved with great artistry. The upper floor could rest solely on these external foundations, and the wooden walls downstairs could be removed without endangering the stability of the building. Hence the name: the house was *umgebunden*, literally 'tied round', or buttressed.

The peak of the linen trade, with which this careful and expensive manner of building was connected, lasted until the end of the eighteenth century. Then American cotton and English mechanical looms swept over the continent and undermined the economic basis of the linen industry in Oberlausitz. The linen weavers did not have the money to change to more modern production methods and the factors failed to organize themselves and adapt in time to the new ideas. As a consequence they lost their wealth within a few generations; they were reduced to working their small holdings and many of their stately buttressed houses fell into ruin. Today those that have survived are among the treasures which this part of eastern Germany has to offer.

Above A colourful chest and other ornaments in a corner of one of the bedrooms.

Left Part of the first floor landing, which contains a variety of traditional furniture including pine chairs and painted chests and cupboards.

Opposite Two exterior views of the *Umgebindehaus* show the wooden arcading on the ground floor that supports the walls and gives the house its name, since it was literally 'tied round' or buttressed.

Left A corner of the kitchen, where the present owner has built this pine cupboard to fit the original alcove, using an old painted door found in the stable of a neighbour's house.

Opposite Another part of the first-floor landing with more examples of traditional furniture including a wooden spinning wheel.

DETAILS

A detail can reveal the character and vitality of a nation's culture, whether it is the superb craftsmanship of a carved oak cabinet in Münster town hall (opposite) or the sculptural virtuosity of a Baroque window surround (above) in Füssen, Bavaria.

Above right A row of stylized heads decorate the medieval portal to the cemetery in Landshut, Bavaria.

Right Late Gothic doorway in Rudolstadt, Thuringia.

Below Doors to the staircase tower at Schloss Münden, near Kassel, Hesse.

DOORS AND WINDOWS

A stylistic period can often best be recognized by its windows or doors. Practical necessity, technical developments, building experience and the spirit of the time all help to determine these very prominent parts of a building. The first stone structures were defensive. They had massive walls, tiny doors and windows cut vertically so that they were hardly visible. But during the Middle Ages walls gradually began to present a different aspect, to display a façade, and windows and doors acquired an aesthetic value in addition to their practical significance.

Windows were important: northern Europe had to manage without the extravagant light of the south. For this reason the amount of light a building let in was increased by enlarging the window opening on the outside and not the inside of the wall. The small round-arched windows could then catch oblique sun rays as well and direct them into the dark rooms. The visual effect on the façade is considerable. The oblique framing lends the wall a majestic and dignified appearance, while the viewer's gaze is drawn to the window by the angled perspective.

In the Romanesque period the portal acquired the form it was to retain throughout the Middle Ages. Church doors had a horizontal lintel across the top, and above the opening was a closed arched area known as the tympanum, which was filled with stone reliefs on religious themes. The whole development of medieval stone carving can be followed on these tympana. In the early Romanesque period the reliefs are static and formalized; Christ is shown with raised hands, a halo and a sublime expression. The reliefs do not yet look sculptural, more like raised icons.

The entrance to the town hall in Pössneck, Thuringia. Constructed between 1478 and 1531, it marks a transition from Gothic to Renaissance styles, with ogee arch windows below and rounded arches above.

Left Elaborate Renaissance ornamentation on the doors of a town house in Duderstadt, Lower Saxony.

Below A less sophisticated entrance, also from the Renaissance period, at Burkheim, near Freiburg im Breisgau, with similarities to Weser Renaissance work.

Above The Renaissance doorway of the town hall in Arnstadt, Thuringia.

Right Doorway of a small house in Waltersdorf, south-east Saxony. The local sandstone used here, being fairly soft and easily carved, gave ample scope for finely sculpted detail.

Far right Entrance to the Baroque Franciscan monastery in Warendorf, near Münster, North Rhine-Westphalia. The contrast of the ornate door surround with the almost severe simplicity of an adjacent window can often be seen on exteriors of this period.

Right Crisp lines and strong colours characterize the door of a town house in Comthurhof, Erfurt.

The parish church in Landsberg am Lech, Bavaria, was originally built in the fifteenth century. Into one of its Gothic door openings has been fitted a pair of richly decorated Baroque doors, in keeping with the impressive Baroque interior.

At the height of the Gothic period reliefs on tympana were highly sculptural, vivid and lifelike, despite the shallowness of the carving. Not only the tympana but also the sides of the portal became more richly ornamented at this time. They were cut obliquely into the walls at even greater angles than the windows, and the area thus gained was subdivided with columns and decorated with ever greater artistry. The Golden Portal of Freiberg cathedral in Saxony has stone carvings of figures from the Old Testament and the Gospels between richly decorated columns; they are surrounded by animals' heads and human faces.

At the same time, in the thirteenth and fourteenth centuries, windows had undergone considerable development. Imperial palaces and princely castles of the Romanesque period had subdivided their walls with small columns and bands of arcades, and the town halls and patrician houses in the towns had opened their interiors to the daylight and air with double or triple windows. Timber frameworks and stone rib vaults made it possible to introduce larger openings into buildings. On church walls these were subdivided with tracery and filled with coloured glass. In secular buildings they were still filled with parchment, wood or oiled linen; glazed windows were more rare.

During the Renaissance architects went back to the forms of antiquity – columns, pilasters, cornices, gables and niches, providing a balanced architecture with a return to the human scale. The visual importance of the window was increased, while the opening itself was actually somewhat reduced. Special attention was given to the portal. The German Renaissance differed from its Italian model in the eagerness with which decorative elements were used, particularly in the design of doors. Stone columns would be scalloped and indented, as if they were wrought-iron candelabra, or receive diagonal serrations and bands as if decorated with iron fittings. Richly embellished friezes, cartouches, animals' bodies, grotesques and graphic designs, steps or flights of stairs – nothing was too much to make the magnificent portal stand out.

In the Baroque period windows lost some of their internal divisions and the sculptural element of the previous period was further increased. Oval or, in southern Germany, curved windows helped to give the walls exuberance and rhythm. The portals were richly articulated, with moulded and figured pediments or supported by hermae. In the Neo-Baroque period of the nineteenth century windows and doors again took on an almost ceremonial importance, but after that the relationship between the wall and its openings was reversed: on the exteriors of the great factory and office buildings of the twentieth century not much has remained of the wall but the steel supports. Architecture of glass, steel and concrete has robbed the individual window of its significance, and fenestration now extends in long rows right across the building. The front has become a single curtain wall of windows stretching from one side to the other. The ultimate development is to make the whole façade a window or the window a façade, and many modern buildings are robed in glass like a reflecting skin.

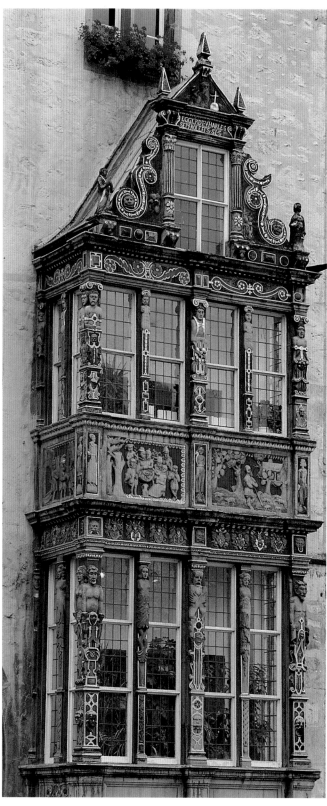

Left A Renaissance bay window (1591), which is attached to the earlier Temple House in Hildesheim, Lower Saxony.

Far left A delicately engraved two-storey Renaissance oriel window on the façade of Landshut town hall.

Right The façade of the Taxis House (1747) in Neuburg an der Donau, Bavaria.

Left Window decoration on the eighteenth-century façade of the Residence in Berchtesgaden, Bavaria.

Right Windows and shutters of a restored seventeenth-century farmhouse at Rudolstadt, Thuringia.

Below Typical wooden-framed and shuttered windows on one of the older houses in Oberammergau, Bavaria.

Above Finely detailed net curtain in the window of a house in Obercunnersdorf, south-east Saxony.

Left Windows with *trompe l'oeil* surrounds (1807; restored 1968–70) on a town house façade in Neuburg an der Donau, Bavaria.

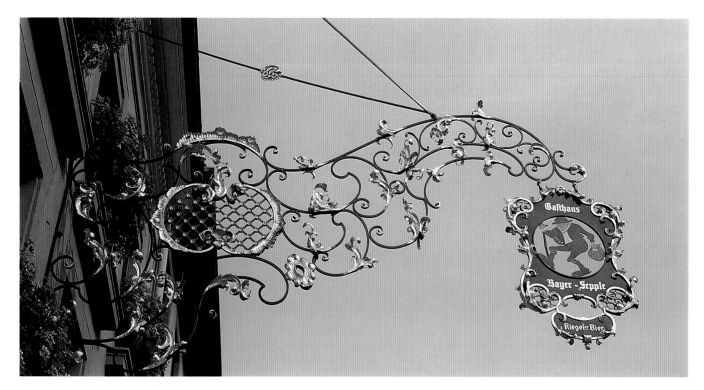

Elaborate wrought-iron, shop and inn signs are very common, especially in the Black Forest area. These are at Waldkirch, near Emmendingen, outside a guest-house (left) and the Duck's Nest Restaurant (below).

METALWORK

Metalwork, particularly ironwork, can like other aspects of German history be considered as starting with Charlemagne. In 774 Charlemagne defeated Desiderius, King of the Langobardi, took his lands in Upper Italy and set the Iron Crown of the Langobardi upon his head. Many German kings were crowned in the same way, symbolically following Charlemagne. But the real economic importance of iron began in the high Middle Ages. The Germans dug deep and searched their mountains for metals earlier and with more determination than many other peoples. The exploitation of mineral resources proved so profitable that associations were formed and large trading companies took shares in them. Rich deposits of ores were found in many districts, and in all of them the land suffered from the disfigurement caused by the ruthless extraction. However, other countries, like Scotland, were impressed by German achievements, and they invited German mining experts to prospect for ores and help develop the mining industry in their own lands.

Iron is a hard metal but it can be fired and shaped, and it quickly became indispensable, not only for warfare but in daily life as well. People asked to enter a house by banging with an iron doorknocker. Those who knocked on a church door were granted protection from their pursuers. Iron was shaped into stands or round holders for candles, it held torches or lanterns and lit the knights' halls. Iron fenders kept the glowing embers in the hearth; chests and doors had iron fastenings and hinges, and iron caskets, keys and locks kept possessions secure.

In the sixteenth century smiths created fine weapons and armour. Curved iron signs outside entrances announced a guild house or inn. During the late Gothic period iron was used to make trellis gates and well-heads, which did not block the view and had simple geometric shapes or naturalistic motifs. Ever since, wrought iron has been used in every period and style where it was desired to close something off but not block the view. Every age fashioned metal in the forms which expressed its interests and concerns, whether as an iron gate or a choir screen, as a window grille or balustrade. The dark, brittle material would adapt to any mode and offered a wide range of expression. On the drawbridges and gates of old castles it looked forbidding and unbeatable, a quality reflected in phrases like the 'Iron Chancellor' or the 'Iron Curtain'.

The Renaissance and Baroque periods showed to what heights of artistry wrought ironwork can be taken. A wrought-iron screen was often placed in a church to separate the choir from the nave without visually breaking the link between the two, and it could serve as a protective fence around reliquaries and fonts. But wrought iron was not only used in churches; the architects of the palaces and residences loved it because it offered both aesthetic and practical values. Used as a banister it gave support to a staircase, while its curves and lines added to the dynamic upward movement of the steps. Outside, massive iron bars at the entrance to the palace drive emphasized the dignity and power of the ruler, without blocking a view of his person or preventing him from looking out. In Baroque churches the iron railing is an important component. It confronts the viewer as soon as he enters, standing between the porch and the great nave. Its beauty makes us forget that it is here for protection and order.

In their simplicity the customary wrought-iron crosses on graves in Saxony and Brandenburg are impressive and moving in a different way. In 1811 an iron monument was set up for Queen Luise in Gransee near Potsdam – wrought iron to honour a queen who was loved for her grace and simple ways,

her liberal convictions and above all her warm-hearted loyalty when her people were in danger. Prussia's misfortunes came from Napoleon, who crushed the Prussian army in 1806.

After that defeat a new type of ironwork became popular. An innovatory casting technique had been developed in Berlin, enabling filigree decorations and jewellery to be made from iron. They combined the dark, silky shimmer of cast iron with an entrancing softness and playfulness. Brooches, hair combs, earrings, necklaces, bracelets and rings were made in the new style, and in the current fashion for French it became known as *fer de Berlin*. In a patriotic fervour during the Wars of Liberation against Napoleon many Prussians gave their gold jewellery to the state between 1813 and 1815 to finance their forces, exchanging it for *fer de Berlin*. Where there was sufficient space on the iron jewellery, the words 'I gave gold for iron' were engraved. The symbolic significance and beauty of the pieces made them increasingly popular, and the Berlin iron foundries went over to mass production. When the iron jewellery was shown at the World Exhibition in London in 1851, the peak of its popularity was already past, but today the old Berlin iron pieces are again eagerly sought by collectors.

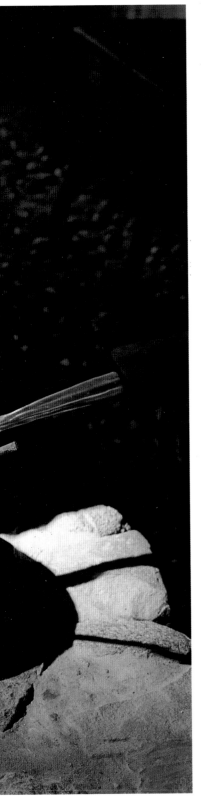

Metals of various kinds were also used to make a variety of functional, everyday objects, including cooking utensils like the traditional copper pots (left); door handles like the witty example (above) from the Renaissance-period Haus zum Palmbaum in Arnstadt, Thuringia; fireplace furniture like the grate supports and coal scuttle (right) from Lüneburg town hall; door hinges like the elaborate Renaissance-period example (far right) from Wasserburg am Inn, Bavaria; and even water spouts like the one (above right) in the font of the Baroque parish church at Landsberg am Lech, Bavaria.

Left and right The façade of this Neo-Baroque town house (about 1900) at Freiburg im Breisgau, is almost overwhelmed by the elaborate wrought ironwork of the gates (detail left) and windows.

Below left Detail of the wrought-iron railings on the entrance steps of the Villa Grisebach, Berlin.

Below and below right Two sections of the cast-iron balustrade on Schinkel's Schlossbrücke (1819–24), near the Altes Museum in Berlin.

Detail of the gates of the AEG Factory, Berlin.

Above and left Wood was used throughout traditional Black Forest houses as can be seen in the bedroom (above) and the *Stube*, or 'living room' (left), of the Resenhof at Bernau.

Opposite Decoration would often be applied to wooden cupboards like the example (above) in the corner of a *Stube* of a former farmhouse near Wolfratshausen, Bavaria, and the late-eighteenth-century wedding cupboard (below) in a small house in the Black Forest. The latter would have been given by the parents to the bride, whose name is at the top, for the storage of linen. Underneath the cupboard in the picture above is a traditional spinning chair, made with only one arm to give more freedom of movement.

WOOD

Near Münster in Westphalia there is a fine country house surrounded by old trees, called Rüschhaus, which was built in the eighteenth century. Later the nineteenth-century writer Annette von Droste-Hülshoff wrote her dark, mystic stories there. She possessed an old table that preoccupied her for many years. Its top is inlaid with a mosaic of two hundred tiny wooden squares. Each is a different wood with its own typical grain. There are native and foreign woods – larch, pine, oak, ash, maple, walnut, birch and rosewood. Each is shown in several variants and colours, including white, yellow, red, grey, brown and black, and each square contains an intricate landscape of lines and whorls that make up the grain of the wood.

It is evident that wood is a highly individual and complicated material, and it is this wealth that makes the history of Western furniture interesting. In Germany the story begins in the early Middle Ages, when houses were still small and internal walls were made of wooden boards. There was not much room for furniture, and the main items were chests and stools. Until the end of the fourteenth century relatively uniform chairs and benches were in use all over the German area. These simple but strong products continued to be used as farm furniture with few changes until well into the nineteenth century.

The chests were long, clumsy boxes, and particularly in the west of Germany they were richly decorated with iron bands.

When the Gothic style in architecture spread from France throughout Christian Europe in the thirteenth century, church furniture typically was the first to change. The choir stalls, prayer stools and pulpits followed the architecture of the church, using pointed arches, buttresses and richly carved tracery. Household furniture remained solid, in the old Romanesque way, for several generations to come. Then the fronts of chests were decorated with early Gothic ornamentation. In the late Gothic period towns grew as trade developed and flourished. The standard of living improved and furniture became more varied, rich and elegant. The cupboard began to compete with the chest and chairs became more comfortable, with arms and a back. Regional differences began to emerge.

In northern Europe oak predominated. Its hard wood resisted carving, but it could be planed. Planing gave rise to the decorative technique of linenfold, which gave flat wooden surfaces the appearance of folded parchment or linen, though with some artistic carving at the end of each fold. From then on its regular forms decorated the panels of chests, cupboards, walls and church furniture. In southern Germany lighter designs and finer patterns were developed, giving rise to a new range of furniture. South of the River Main carpenters used softer woods like fir and pine, and they were able to give their furniture a more attractive appearance. Surfaces were covered with relief patterns, while stylized foliage was spread luxuriously over the boards and feet.

The free imperial cities in the south of Germany profited from their close trade relations with Upper Italy. Their emerging capitalist culture was similar to that in Italy and it made them receptive to the ideas of the Renaissance. Under its influence they transformed south German furniture. Columns, pilasters, mouldings and gables now enlivened the fronts of furniture here too. Nuremberg pioneered the new trend. The Renaissance cupboards by the Nuremberg master Peter Flötner were still made of pine wood, but they were covered with a veneer of ash and enlivened with relief carvings in lime or oak. Many surfaces were finished with inlays, using thin veneers generally taken from imported woods.

North of the Main furniture developed more

Left Detail of a confessional in St Maria im Kapitol, Cologne. An anthropomorphic rendering of a pensive monkey is surrounded by stylized plants and a bird of prey.

Right One of the wonderfully expressive series of fifteenth-century woodcarvings in the choir of Ulm Cathedral.

Right The Hall of Peace, used as a council chamber, in Münster town hall. Against the wall are document cabinets with unusual early-sixteenth-century carvings. Despite thematic variations they are all considered to be the work of the same craftsman.

Opposite Two of the cabinets in the Hall of Peace. The two headless warriors in the upper panel symbolize destructive and self-destructive war.

slowly. Oak was still preferred, and it was elaborately carved and decorated. In the late sixteenth century carved oak panels were installed in Münster town hall's Hall of Peace; they are covered with linenfold, grotesques, lively ornamentation and figurative representations, which look more like carved pictures than furniture decoration.

In the Baroque period Germany developed a preference for monumental scale and excessive decoration, influenced by the desire of absolutist rulers for ostentation. The differences between north and south Germany that had been evident until then in the choice of wood for furniture became less marked, but dividing lines did remain, only now they were between the principalities and the great trading centres. Walnut veneers became popular, as their fine-pored, elegantly grained, matt surfaces met the need of the time for costly effect. Then in the nineteenth century walnut trees were ravaged by a sequence of bad winters, and walnut gave way to mahogany.

The courts of a number of eighteenth-century principalities vied with each other to be the most inventive and original, but among them the courts of the Bavarian elector at Munich and of Frederick the Great at Berlin and Potsdam stood out as centres for luxury furniture. The softer forms of furniture suited the more refined taste. With great delicacy and sensitivity wall decorations were enlivened with typical Rococo motifs drawn from nature, such as flowers, fruit and birds, as well as with musical instruments. The Rococo taste loved exotic, multicoloured woods like rose, lemon or violet wood, from which diamond or chequer-board patterns were cut or garlands of flowers twisted.

After the Napoleonic Wars a particular style in furniture, Biedermeier, developed under English influence and using the language of Classical architecture. The middle class wanted furniture to be both dignified and comfortable. In addition to the popular mahogany, birch, ash, pear and cherry were favourite veneers. In the second half of the century old-fashioned wood, particularly oak, came back into use with the historicist movement.

If Annette von Droste-Hülshoff could sit down at a table today whose top was made of all the materials now available, she would no doubt be amazed at its range and variety. The number of natural and artificial materials with which we surround ourselves is so great it can hardly be listed.

Above Detail of the wood inlay decoration on the walls of the Small Marquetry Chamber in the Neue Kammern at Sanssouci, Potsdam. The effect is mainly achieved by using different coloured woods.

Right Similar but more delicately executed decoration in the Registry Office of the new town hall at Freiburg im Breisgau, Baden-Württemberg.

Right The staircase in the late-nineteenth-century Villa Grisebach in Fasanenstrasse, Berlin, and a detail (below) showing a putto. It was expertly restored in 1985.

Far right Here carving and inlay work (about 1900) are used together to almost grotesque effect in the Assembly Room of Freiburg's new town hall.

COLOURS

Colours are important for the Germans, as their language shows, for of all the world languages German is the only one with a single, common word for a variety of colours – *bunt*. In English this is translated as 'multi-coloured' and in French 'multi-colore'. In Germany nothing can be done without at least some theory, and German colour theory would be inconceivable without Johann Wolfgang von Goethe, who was concerned with how we see colour and the relationship of colours to light.

Although he was already at the height of his fame as a writer, Goethe at times devoted himself entirely to the natural sciences. In 1810 he published his theory of colour in the form of a sharp attack on Newton, although by then Newton had been dead for nearly a hundred years. Perhaps the controversy was quite unnecessary, for Goethe and Newton seem to have been exploring different things: Newton studied colours in the dark room and evolved an analytical, abstract theory of colour; Goethe, who used the visual approach, would not accept anything he could not see with his naked eye. He wanted to understand the visual qualities of colours and their differences and so arrive at an order that could be sensually perceived. How much more telling it is to explain the rainbow and the psychological effect of colours, as Goethe did, without using the language of mathematics, and to imagine that light and darkness are battling in colour. Goethe conducted an impassioned campaign against the scientists, including those of

Left Part of the Romanesque paintings on the ceiling of the nave in St Michael's Church, Hildesheim, Lower Saxony. This remarkable series was designed to provide a family tree of the Old Testament, from Adam and Eve at the west end to Christus Pantokrator in the east. Here the figure of King Joshua in the centre is surrounded by four lesser kings and, at the sides, four prophets.

Opposite Detail of the medieval wall paintings in the dressing room at Burg Eltz, Rhineland-Palatinate. The soft range of colours in which the fantastical, stylized flowers and leaves now appear may originally have been much brighter.

Left Red brick and red tiles are very much a feature of northern Germany, and especially on buildings in Lüneburg, such as the town hall (left) and a town house (right) on the main square (Am Sande).

his own day, and he would have liked, he said, to see 'their donkey's ears nailed to their desks'.

Goethe's theory of colour is certainly closer to art than to science, and in art, of course, colour plays a major part. Here we can only touch on a few, very subjective chords in the great symphonies of colour that have been composed over centuries in the churches, monasteries, palaces, town halls, cities and villages of Germany. We first encounter colour as a means of design in German art in the Romanesque wall paintings found in churches and monasteries. From time to time restoration work in the smaller churches uncovers more of these under layer after layer of paint. They have always been visible in the great Romanesque churches of the Rhineland, such as St Maria in Lyskirchen in Cologne or the double church of Schwarzrheindorf near Bonn. Today these wall paintings seem delicate and pastel-coloured, but at the time, as medieval book illustrations suggest,

their colours were probably strong and fresh. The size of the painting on the wall of the church must have created a rich and luminous effect.

The Gothic period added light to colour as stained glass windows took over the role of wall paintings. They let daylight in to the high church nave through tinted panes, and their colours glowed. A different colour effect was created by sculptors and stone-masons in the thirteenth century. Capitals and arches were decorated with carved and painted stone reliefs often depicting a variety of plant forms. In Altenberg cathedral in Bergisches Land the capitals are still painted in powerful naturalistic colours, and in Naumburg cathedral there are remarkable sculpted and painted stone figures, whose colours have faded with age. But the faces, the clothes, even the stone arches over the heads of the figures, must once have been strongly coloured as powerfully and movingly as the feelings the faces display.

The Gothic period was also the great age of brick building, and brick was used wherever natural stone was not available. Fired into various shades of red, bricks determine the colour of buildings in the north, from the Netherlands to the Baltic. The Romanesque period had built strongly, massively and close to the earth. Now, in the Gothic period, the churches, city towers, halls and fortifications seemed to stretch up into the sky, as if reaching ever upwards. The master builders of Brick Gothic emphasized this upward-striving movement by arranging differently fired and reddened bricks in vertical rows, one beside the next. They subdivided the façades, sent the buildings soaring into the air and gave the material an entrancing, weightless quality.

The Renaissance brought richly decorated portals, coloured in red, blue, green and gold. In the south the influence of Italian colour is still evident, while in the north the tones are rather cooler and softer. Some

Above Red-roofed houses and narrow streets are tightly packed together in the historic north German town of Celle, Lower Saxony.

Left Red brick can also be effective in a half-timbered setting, as in this typical Wendland barn at Damnatz, Lower Saxony, on the Elbe.

Above and left The façade of the Wedekind House in Hildesheim (above) – originally built in 1598, then restored after the Second World War – and the main doors of Münden town hall (left), built in 1605, exemplify the polychromatic decoration of the German Renaissance, especially in the north.

Right Renaissance wall-painting in the *Gerichtslaube* of Lüneburg town hall: the rich blues and reds of the Justice Picture (top) are echoed in the arches below, and merge into the predominantly gold colour scheme of the walls.

Left Part of the grotto complex at Schloss Neuburg an der Donau, Bavaria, with signs of the zodiac depicted on the ceiling. The relief images are built up of small shells, set against a vivid azure ground representing the cosmos. The original date of this decoration is uncertain, but stylistically it exemplifies the practice, fairly common in Germany from the sixteenth to the nineteenth centuries, of following Italian Renaissance models.

Above right Decoratively framed painting on the wall of St Quirin (1684–9) in Tegernsee, Bavaria.

Above far right A painted doorway in the staircase hall of Gengenbach abbey, Baden-Württemberg, illustrates the brilliance (and wit) of *trompe l'oeil* painting during the Baroque period.

Renaissance façades were left without much colour, but often walls and ceilings inside were wonderfully decorated and magnificently painted. The greatest symphonies in colour were done during the Baroque age, when the interiors of churches from Bohemia to the Rhineland reflected the triumphant art of the Counter-Reformation. In the halls and staircases of Baroque palaces walls were dissolved with the help of illusionistic, and often architectural, *trompe l'oeil* paintings. In the Rococo period colours became light and delicate, and they can be seen at their finest in the white and gold of the Wies church in Bavaria, which has just been restored to its original colouring.

Neoclassicism in Germany enlivened its interiors with the colours of Pompeii and Herculaneum. Karl Friedrich Schinkel loved to use brilliant colours in the interior – bright or dark green, blue, red and a strong yellow – to set against his off-white façades. This scheme has been impressively realized in the Charlottenhof palace in Potsdam.

At the end of the nineteenth century the generation of the *Gründerjahre* period, the years when German industry was being established, wanted stately, pompous colours. It seemed as if the easier it became to make colours industrially, the more their effect had to be intensified. The plants in parks and gardens also had to be voluptuous, and the bushy, strongly coloured rhododendron was particularly popular at this time. The Jugendstil, or Art Nouveau, period brought a counter-movement, with a preference for natural, finer, more delicate tones and less ostentatious plants. Wild roses, open, unfilled blossoms, sinewy climbers, simple conifers, a pale young birch in a light-coloured heathland or on a brown moor suited the cooler Jugendstil tones.

To conclude this brief survey let us take a quick look at the German national colours – black-red-gold. Black and red were the colours of the Holy Roman Empire, which was dissolved in 1806 by Napoleon. Black became the symbol of the German freedom fighters against Napoleon; the famous Lützow Jäger, or riflemen, were the first to wear it in battle and they called it their 'robe of vengeance'. But actually black was chosen for a practical reason – the soldiers in the Wars of Liberation, or Napoleonic Wars, were not a professional army, they were a volunteer force. They had to pay for their own uniforms, and as black was the cheapest dye they chose that as their troop colour. Their uniforms consisted of civilian coats dyed black, with red braiding and gold buttons added. This is how black-red-gold became the symbol of the fight for democracy and national German unity.

After the Second World War both German states chose the same combination of colours for their national flags. The GDR, however, added the socialist symbols, the hammer, sickle and wreath of corn, and the old symbol of unity became a bitter demonstration of the division of Germany. Then in 1989 came the peaceful revolution in the GDR, when hundreds of thousands of people poured onto the streets of Leipzig, Dresden and Berlin to protest at Communist rule. They cut out the socialist symbols from the GDR flag, leaving only the colours that had accompanied the fight for a democratic and unified Germany nearly two hundred years before.

Above and left The delicate colours of the Rococo period: a corner of the staircase hall in St Peter's monastery, near Freiburg im Breisgau, Baden-Württemberg (above), and part of the ceiling of the Wies church, in Bavaria (left).

Opposite above Sensuous gold-painted reliefs representing scenes from Greek mythology dominate the Ovid Gallery in the late Rococo Neue Kammern at Sanssouci, Potsdam. This one is of Pomona and Vertumnus.

Opposite below In the guest room at the west end of the Neue Kammern pink walls are superbly set off by the green mouldings, curtains and upholstery, while the wooden parquet floor turns gold in the afternoon sun.

Details from Neoclassical *Bildtapete* (pictorial wall-paper) in a town house in Warendorf, near Münster. Of French origin, they are a striking example of the foreign influences to which German culture has always been subject. In the Garden Room (right) are scenes from the eighteenth-century French novel *The Incas or the Destruction of the Peruvian Empire*. The subject matter in the Saloon (below) is derived from *Telemach on the Island of Calypso*, a popular psychological novel of the time.

Part of the Neo-Rococo Malachitzimmer in the orangery at Sanssouci, Potsdam. The name of the room is derived from the dark-green stone used for the fireplace, which comes from Malachit in the Ural Mountains of Russia and was a gift from the Tsar.

Above Modern stained glass in the restored *Gerichtslaube* (law court) in the original town hall building at Freiburg im Breisgau, Baden-Württemberg, seems to achieve the brilliant colours of medieval originals.

Left Red and gold are the dominant colours in the coats of arms (probably nineteenth-century) of the local nobility, displayed in the Old Customs House at Freiburg im Breisgau.

In the town hall at Landshut, Bavaria, a magnificent frieze of nineteenth-century paintings commemorates the wedding procession of the Duke of Landshut in 1475, when he married the daughter of the King of Poland. This scene shows the Emperor Frederick III of Hapsburg, accompanied by his page. The procession is still re-enacted in the town today, every fourth year, with 2500 participants in costumes made to the original medieval patterns.

The façades of buildings throughout Germany display the most varied colour schemes: blue-grey tiles on a village house in Obercunnersdorf, Saxony (above); red-ochre on the exterior of the Old Customs House in Freiburg im Breisgau (right); contrasting blue and pink on two town houses in Landshut (opposite above); yellow for the nineteenth-century Villa Lingg overlooking Lake Constance (opposite below left); and an unusual mixture of green, yellow, purple and blue for the Neue Staatsgalerie in Stuttgart (opposite below right).

LÜFTLMALEREI

Bavaria is farmyard Italy, said the theatre critic Alfred Kerr; here you can find Latin art forms created by villagers. The brightly coloured paintings on the fronts of houses in the Lower Alps, known as *Lüftlmalerei*, do indeed have a delightfully naive quality. They are naive in expression, choice of colours and themes, but not necessarily in artistic merit, for they may be very skilfully painted.

The artists of these house fronts were experts at handling perspective and movement, and they have succeeded in creating the illusion of three-dimensional stucco, with windows, doors, columns, architraves, niches, portals, stairs and balustrades all depicted on a façade. Sometimes people are to be seen looking out of windows that do not exist at all, and they seem to be looking at the observer who is looking at them. These simple but masterful pictures are as characteristic of the Lower Alps as the onion towers on the churches. They have a southern charm, and they do distantly recall the proud frescoes on the patrician houses of the rich Italian trading cities.

The relationship is historical. Between the steep walls of the Karwendel and Wetterstein mountains lay the great trade route that has led since Roman times from Italy through the Brenner pass and Innsbruck to Partenkirchen and Augsburg in the north. In the Middle Ages, too, Italian goods rolled over the Alps on wagons, to be reloaded on to rafts on the Bavarian side and steered down the Isar to Munich and Landshut. They were golden times for Upper Bavaria as the maritime Republic of Venice secured its monopoly of trade with the orient. Even after the goods had taken other routes, Bavaria retained its prosperity, and with it the popular art of house painting. The proximity to Italy is also evident in the religion here, and all over rural Bavaria you notice the colourful and pious presence of the Catholic faith. In the Protestant north you would not expect to find brightly coloured pictures of the Virgin Mary and the saints painted all over the fronts of houses.

The painters of these house fronts used the same fresco technique as their Italian masters. A fine plaster paste is spread on a façade; this serves as a background for the picture, which has to be painted quickly and with a sure hand, in mineral paints, before the plaster dries. As it dries the plaster

Above The Hospital Church at Füssen: the fully decorated façade of this small Baroque building, with its central coat of arms and flanking figures of saints, is an outstanding example of Bavarian *Lüftlmalerei*.

Left Part of the old town hall in Bamberg, which illustrates the three-dimensional architectural effect that can be achieved by this method of decoration.

mingles with the paint to form a solid layer that is resistant to rain and snow.

Lüftlmalerei reached its peak in the eighteenth century, but the people in this region are still having pictures of saints, ornaments or flower decoration painted on the façades of their houses, and the same technique is used. Favourite subjects are biblical themes, illustrated with a childlike reverence. Sometimes their effect is heightened by a detailed background of simulated architecture, while words in banners underneath add to the clarity. Protective saints and other tutelary spirits float beside windows, warding off fire, sickness and famine. Everyday life also finds expression, including hunts and hunters, wild animals and livestock, barking dogs, hens and goats, wagons and cracking whips. In short, it can be confirmed that Bavaria really is a farmyard Italy.

Left Two façades in Wallgau, a Bavarian village near Garmisch-Partenkirchen.

Opposite Detail of the façade of the Hirsch Apotheke in the fish market, Offenburg (Baden-Württemberg). Here the design is engraved as well as painted.

Below left The façade of the Pilatushaus at Oberammergau, Bavaria, provides a striking example of *trompe l'oeil*.

Below The massive Renaissance wall-painting above the Bridge Gate in Wasserburg am Inn, Bavaria, showing two men in armour holding Bavarian and Wasserburg banners.

TOWNS

*Germany's historical division into a large number of
independent states, each with their own urban centres, has
left the country with many long-established towns, which,
like Freudenberg (opposite) in North Rhine-Westphalia or
Schmalkalden (above) in Thuringia, still retain a strong
traditional atmosphere, often with a wealth of half-
timbered buildings.*

It is in the smaller towns that you have the impression of being right in the middle of Germany – in the old, original Germany. That is not to criticize the great metropolises, those massive, complicated and fascinating nerve centres. But in the small towns one is still much more aware of the natural community rooted in village life. The link with the landscape has not been broken, and the people have not lost sight of wood and pasture, lake and river. The traditional appearance of their locality gives them a feeling of security. They share a community life and feel bound by local traditions.

The large German cities also still betray their village past. Even in Berlin, truly an international city, the attentive observer will see that it only began to eat its way into its surrounding meadows, pastures, sandy soil and lakes in the nineteenth century, swallowing many a village in the marshes in the process. The district of Kladow on the Havel, which grew up from a Slav settlement, and Marienfelde, founded by the Knights Templar in the thirteenth century, have retained their old village centres and their one-storey farm houses with timber cladding, wooden shutters and flower gardens.

Smaller towns like Bamberg, Landshut, Königslutter, Duderstadt and Wernigerode still show their traditional charm much more clearly. Winding streets, rows of houses and a centre that has developed organically are doubly delightful because they recall their past but are still inhabited, quite normally and without any particular show.

East Germany is nowhere so delightful as in its smaller towns. How attractive, touching in a rather melancholy way, is their old-fashioned beauty, although it is the enforced result of lack of economic development. At the moment most people seem to think of East Germany as the sleeping beauty, just awakening to new life under the kisses of the rich princes from West Germany. In the fairytale the sleeping girl stayed young for a hundred years, but in reality the towns and villages of the GDR were gradually decaying in a period of decline and neglect that lasted four decades. It is not possible to foresee today whether the neglect of the past can be made good.

The essential character of any town is determined by its history. Many towns are so young that they are still in their first peak. Others are fortunate enough to have been noteworthy in every period of history. They were great and powerful centuries ago and are

Germany's smaller towns often possess much old-fashioned charm. Celle (left) in Lower Saxony, with its atmospheric Zollnerstrasse (right) is a good example of this as are Burkheim (below) in Baden-Württemberg and Warendorf (below right) in North Rhine-Westphalia.

Overleaf The medieval towers and old houses of Rothenburg ob der Tauber, Bavaria, seem rooted in the surrounding landscape.

even more so today. This is where the old mingles with the new, often in unequal parts. But there are also towns that flourished and were then forgotten by history, so they have been able to retain their old features. Anyone who studies the development of a town or city, its architecture and layout as well as its connection with the landscape, will learn much about its earlier identity.

Bamberg in Upper Franconia, for instance, is an ecclesiastical city. In 1007 the German King and later Emperor Heinrich II founded a bishopric there, and it grew to be one of the richest and most powerful in

the land. Located at the junction of the Rivers Main and Regnitz, the town developed into a major religious and cultural centre in the early Middle Ages. It was the burial place of Clemens II, the only pope buried on German soil. Bamberg's older medieval parts stretch from the river, in a picturesque sweep uphill. The streets run in all directions, nestling against the hill, seemingly without planning or design. Towering above it all is the mighty early Gothic cathedral on the hill. This higher part of the

town is the religious quarter, and it is still the seat of the archbishop. Several former monasteries are also to be found here. Down on the other side of the river is the district where the citizens, the craftsmen and merchants, used to live. The old town hall dates from the fourteenth century, and it formed the link between the town and the bishop's quarter, serving as a bridge and a gate between the two parts of the town.

Gengenbach, nestling in the foothills of the Black Forest, is a small German provincial town today. It

grew up in the fertile old settlement area of the Upper Rhine plain. In the eighth century Benedictine monks founded an abbey there, and the monastery church still dominates the confusion of old streets and alleyways. Gengenbach's great period began in the fourteenth century, when the German towns became the third estate of the Holy Roman Empire, after the church and the great landowners. Gengenbach became a free imperial town, directly under the emperor and not a landowner, and with a seat in the

Left Two views of the old town hall in Bamberg, which is an unusual mixture of Rococo and much earlier half-timbered work and is perhaps the most striking municipal building in Germany. It is dramatically situated on an island in the river, which divides the civic and ecclesiastical parts of the town.

Opposite left Like other old German towns, Bamberg has many narrow, crooked alleyways, that can only be explored on foot. Here a steep flight of steps leads down into Hinterer Bach, which eventually rises again to the cathedral in the background.

Gengenbach in the Black Forest is one of Germany's more picturesque towns, with numerous half-timbered houses and narrow cobbled passages as well as an old well.

In season, much of Gengenbach, including squares and fountains, is covered with a profusion of flowers and plants, which hang from window-boxes or grow against walls, softening the black-and-white effect of the half-timbering.

Reichstag. The huge gate towers in the city fortifications date from this period. It is a small place with a great past.

The system by which the early emperors ruled influenced the evolution of many towns in the Middle Ages. They did not have a fixed residence that could have developed into a capital city but ruled the land from fortified seats scattered throughout their territory. The emperor travelled continuously with his court from one of these imperial seats to the next, and so embellished cities with wonderful Romanesque buildings throughout his realm. Gelnhausen, Worms, Ingelheim, Frankfurt, Forchheim, Quedlinburg, Magdeburg, Goslar and Cologne are some of these; most important was Aachen.

We know little about everyday life in the early Middle Ages and what we know seems both picturesque and uncomfortable. Small wooden houses squatted in the shadow of the castles and imperial palaces. Their walls were made of clay and straw and the roofs were covered with reed thatch or shingle, so they were easily inflammable. And most of them did burn down. The living rooms and sleeping quarters do not seem to have been separated and there was hardly any furniture. Only one central room was heated, so it must have been terribly cold in these houses. People slept in the clothes they wore during the day. Only the wall-hangings and carpets that were intended to keep out the cold brought a little comfort into the bare rooms.

In the twelfth century towns developed rapidly. The commercial production of glass, textiles and metal goods began, long-distance trade flourished and the standard of living and people's requirements grew. With their new-found strength the towns challenged the central powers, the church and the secular rulers. 'Town air is free', as the saying went, free of the serfdom on the land. This is evident from the Gothic town views. Civic freedom found architectural expression in high walls, clearly separating the town from the land. The free market and trade privileges, perhaps the citizens' ability to defend themselves as well, are symbolized in the old 'Roland' sculptures in wood or stone on the town halls in the north and east of Germany. For a long time it was thought that this knight, depicted with his armour and sword, was the young nephew of Charlemagne, about whom many legends had arisen. He was the hero of the *Rolandslied*, the 'Song of Roland', which the crusaders sang on their way to Jerusalem.

Over the centuries a new class of people slowly grew up in the towns, the bourgeoisie. Their prosperity and influence are evident from the great guild and town halls, and on the skyline the towers of secular buildings rose up beside those of the churches. These buildings had balconies and gables, fine decoration on the façades and high-pitched roofs. The Gürzenich in Cologne (built as a dancing hall for councillors' families) and the town halls in Aachen, Augsburg, Lüneburg and Lübeck all combine the ceremonial magnificence of a public building with the self-confidence of the new merchant class.

Without the organizing, controlling and protective role of the guilds the new middle class could probably not have developed. The guilds were unions of craftsmen formed to supervise markets, control working conditions and fix a 'fair' price for goods. They offered economic security and protection in case of need. They even regulated the moral behaviour and clothing of their members. In the high Middle Ages the guilds controlled almost every aspect of daily life and without their approval it was virtually impossible to live and work in any town. Even beggars and prostitutes had to belong to their own 'guild'. Each guild had a hall, and the buildings

expressed the power and financial strength of the organization. The Butchers' Guildhall in Hildesheim, which was destroyed in the last war, but subsequently restored, and the Cloth Hall in Brunswick are fine examples of north German Renaissance architecture.

In the high Middle Ages towns became an ever more coherent architectural whole. As prosperity grew the middle class could also afford to build stone houses and workshops. The windows still hung somewhat irregularly in the façade, for the outside only reflected the internal structure of the house, but the ground plan gradually extended to include a front building, courtyard and a rear building. Saw mills, first mentioned in a document in 1322, made wood panelling on the walls possible and facilitated the production of furniture. The interiors grew more varied. In the Gothic period narrow vertical façades were still current, rising into filigree-like, stepped gables. Later the Renaissance houses of the bourgeoisie were able to fit harmoniously into the general townscape. Their façades were given a new appearance with wall paintings, oriel windows, richly decorated portals and gables, and other architectural embellishments. In towns like Landshut, Hameln,

Minden and Höxter these stately Renaissance houses still stand, one close to the next.

What has remained of this old urban culture? A few well-preserved streets in some towns, whole quarters in others. Places like Landshut or Bamberg have retained much of the flair of the old period today. Perhaps more has survived than is immediately apparent (because subconsciously it has entered the traditions and way of life): the pride, for instance, and independence of the medieval towns that had freed themselves of territorial rulers and the dominance of the church. The free imperial towns only lost their status when the Holy Roman Empire was dissolved by Napoleon in 1806, and some towns have retained their independence to today. Hamburg and Bremen insist on their title of 'Free Hanseatic Town', and as city states they, like the big states, or *Länder*, send members to the Bundesrat, the Upper Chamber of the Federal German Parliament.

Another heritage of the Middle Ages is half-timbering. This traditional and irregular way of building houses was an unmistakable characteristic of the towns and villages in Germany right up into the twentieth century. The structural principle of half-timbering is very simple. The wooden frame of

Above and above far right The historic town house façades that give Landshut its distinctive character mix different periods and styles in a harmonious fusion, as at Landgasse (above), where the narrow Gothic houses adjoin the more expansive Rococo Etzdorf Palace, and the late Gothic Pappenberg House (far right) on Altstadt.

Above left Two views of Lüneburg, where the emerging bourgeoisie built themselves town houses with particularly striking *Backsteingotik*, or Brick Gothic, gables, especially round the main square (Am Sande).

Above centre The town hall at Landsberg am Lech, Bavaria, by D. Zimmermann (1699–1702). In Germany even important Baroque façades may be adorned by window-boxes.

Left The market square of Hildesheim, with its sixteenth-century guild houses (rebuilt after the Second World War), seen through one of the Gothic arches of the town hall arcade. In the centre is the Butchers' Guildhall with the Bakers' Guild House on the left and the Town Tavern to the right.

Above Mittelstadt, the principal street in the small Kaiserstuhl town of Burkheim, Baden-Württemberg, has a particularly striking example of a half-timbered house (on the left) with an unusual arrangement of beams.

Right A typical half-timbered façade, echoing the colour and the shadows of the adjacent trees, at Münden, on the Weser near Kassel.

the house is set on a rectangle of oaken beams. The open spaces between the beams are filled with a mixture of sticks and clay (wattle and daub), but they could be filled in with natural stone or brick. This method had great advantages. No other material is as flexible and easy to work as wood. Moreover, valuable wood was only needed for the frame of the house, much less than if the house had been solidly constructed. The spaces between could simply be filled with the material that was readily to hand. Only hard, slowly matured oak was stable enough for the frame, for the beams had to be as strong as ship's masts. Carpenters' tools were surprisingly simple. Almost everything on the building was made with an axe, even the conically shaped wooden nails. Only much later did the saw come into use, and this made building considerably easier.

When the house was built the beams were painted or decorated and the infill between whitewashed. It is this contrast between the beams and infill that gives the half-timbered front its particular attraction. In Siegerland, a hilly area in North Rhine-Westphalia, where houses are roofed with black slate, the beams are a deep black and the walls as startlingly white as if the colour had been put on yesterday. In the south the half-timbering has softer contrasts, with warm brown, wooden beams and yellowish or earth-coloured walls. In the north, on the other hand, the walls were usually left unplastered and the bricks are visible. Sometimes the timber beams are actually painted white, to provide a fresh contrast to the red brick walls. On some half-timbered fronts the beams are arranged in strange, irregular patterns, and unusual names have evolved in popular speech to describe particular arrangements of beams, such as 'St Andrew's Cross', 'Wild Man', 'Thunder Broom', 'Mill'. They recall the stories of saints and Grimm's fairytales, and they are as intriguing as the half-timbering itself.

In the first half of the seventeenth century the Thirty Years' War wrought terrible destruction in the towns. When it finally came to an end most of the towns had been plundered and fired and their walls torn apart. Trade and crafts, the basis of urban life, lay in ruins. When the reconstruction work started, conditions had fundamentally changed. The towns were weakened by the peace terms but the princes had emerged with their power greatly strengthened. Consequently, building principles changed during the Baroque period; now the absolutist rulers made

Above The black-and-white contrast of the half-timbering on this house at Warendorf, near Münster, is lightened and varied by the cream and red colour scheme of the windows and shutters in the foreground.

Right Detail of a house in Duderstadt, near Göttingen, Lower Saxony, where the beams have been painted red in a typical example of the polychromatic ornamentation of the German Renaissance.

Above Freudenberg (near Siegen in North Rhine-Westphalia) exemplifies the strong black-and-white contrast of half-timbered work in central and northern towns.

generous plans following the rules of geometry and perspective. Designs became more formal and intended to create an effect. Stone was a more worthy building material and stonemasons and stucco workers replaced the carpenters and wood-carvers. Old towns and cities, like Kassel, Berlin, Dresden and Würzburg, were transformed with new squares and streets into Baroque principalities, and new towns were laid out to formal plans around the rulers' palaces, in keeping with the hierarchical view of the social order.

Mannheim is a striking example of this, but the most outstanding is Karlsruhe, laid out as the seat and centre of government of the Margrave of Baden-Durlach. There are no medieval walls to restrict the city centre here, but from one central place thirty-two streets radiate in a star shape, with a regularity that was quite literally drawn with a ruler on a drawing-board. The streets that lead to the front of the palace contain the town houses, while those behind lead straight into the neighbouring woods, for Karlsruhe was built up on a margrave's hunting lodge. At the junction of the concentric arrangement stands the ruler's magnificent Baroque palace. This is urban planning designed to increase the standing

Schloss Weikersheim, Baden-Württemberg, with its vineyards rising behind it and part of the town in the foreground (right). In 1719 the Renaissance residence was linked to the town's market place by building the two quarter-circle arcaded structures (below).

of the ruler and of the town as a stage for his princely display. The plans and their execution look like chessboards on which people were moved like pawns, and in the rules of this human game each person had only the freedom to play the role that was assigned to him.

Over the ages, churches, princes and the bourgeoisie have clearly left their marks, visible and invisible, on the towns and cities, each in their own way. But the Jewish urban culture has been destroyed and almost completely obliterated in Germany, although it helped to form the face of German towns for centuries. In medieval times they seem themselves to have preferred to live in their own quarters outside the Christian areas, where they could have their synagogue, school, bath house and hospital close together. Evidence of the peaceful coexistence of Jews and Christians at this time is seen in the fact that the same team of builders who built the great Romanesque cathedral in Speyer probably constructed Speyer's Jewish bathhouse, where the Jews performed the ritual washing prescribed in the Talmud.

The Jews also often had citizens' rights until the end of the Middle Ages, when ever stricter rules were introduced, following the demands of the Catholic church, to segregate Jews and Christians. Jews were excluded from the tight status network of Christian guilds and only a few occupations were open to them. As money-lending was abhorred by Christians they could trade and engage in banking, and so they became indispensable to the emperor, the bishops and the city councils. From the time of the crusades the peaceful coexistence of Christians and Jews was disrupted by repeated waves of persecution, and in the fourteenth century, during the Great Plague, terrible riots broke out. The Jews were even more strictly segregated, and by the sixteenth century at the latest the Jewish districts had become ghettos. They were not opened up until the end of the eighteenth, when under the impact of the French Revolution and with the struggle for bourgeois freedoms the Jews also received equal rights.

Today only the cemeteries show that German cities had living, organic Jewish communities for many centuries. The holocaust in the twentieth century almost completely destroyed them. The visitor to a German city today would hardly know what a great culture the Germans had eradicated from their midst.

INDEX

Page numbers in *italic* refer to the illustrations